A Collection from MYSTERIES OF THE UNKNOWN

Visions and Prophecies

Omens and Auguries	4
Portents in the Palm	25
Penmanship and Personality	35
Charting the Four Basic Numbers	40
Casting Your Fate	46
Dominoes and Destiny	48

Psychic Powers

Other Ways of Seeing	52
The World of the Psychic	60
Psychics at Center Stage	81

This booklet has been adapted and produced especially for TIME Magazine by TIME-LIFE BOOKS from the series Mysteries of the Unknown.

Visions and Prophecies

Omens and Auguries

he legend began one night in the early 1600s on the remote Scottish isle of Lewis. According to the traditional account, a hearty Highland woman named Mrs. Mackenzie was grazing her herd of cattle alongside an old graveyard, when all at once the entire crop of tombstones wavered, creaked, and toppled to the ground. As Mrs. Mackenzie watched in frozen fascination, ghosts floated out of the ground and flew swiftly away.

More intrigued than afraid, the Scottish woman waited to see what would happen. An hour later all the ghosts but one had returned from their wanderings in the mortal realm. Mrs. Mackenzie then placed her staff over the last open grave. Finally, the wraith of a young woman appeared and shrieked, "Lift your distaff from my grave and let me enter my dwelling of the dead!" "I shall do so," said the staunch Mrs. Mackenzie, "when you explain to me what detained you so long after your neighbors."

"My journey was much farther than theirs," replied the shade. "I had to go all the way to Norway. I am a daughter of its king and was drowned while bathing. My body was carried out to sea and eventually swept onto the shore not far from here, where it was found and interred in that grave. Now please remove your distaff so that I may once more take my rest."

Mrs. Mackenzie did so, and before the dead princess sank back into the earth, she said, "In remembrance of me, and as a small reward of your courage, I shall tell you where you will find something of rare value. If you will search in that loch over there, you will come across a small round blue stone. Give it to your son, who by it shall see into the future."

Mrs. Mackenzie found the mysterious treasure and presented it to her son. When he peered through a hole in the center of the stone, he found that the phantom had spoken the truth. Using this curious stone, a simple object drawn from nature, he could slice through the veils of time and divine what was to come, thus fulfilling one of humanity's most ancient dreams.

This tale typifies the legends that sprang up around the obscure Renaissance seer Kenneth Mackenzie—or Coinneach Odhar, as he preferred to be called in Gaelic. Very little is known of the man himself, but records of the sixteenth-century Scottish parliament contain an order, sent to authorities in the county of Ross, to prosecute the wizard Coinneach Odhar. Presumably, this led to his execution. And it would not be surprising if his crime had been the widespread practice of scrying—divination by gazing into shining surfaces. Nor would it be unusual for a man of that era to claim second sight, an ability that many Scots still believe to be their birthright. The wizard of parliamentary record differs from the story's prophet in one key aspect, however: He lived almost a century before the events related in the Coinneach Odhar legend, a fact that only adds to the mystery surrounding him.

The seer was said to have announced his prophecies in a manner that daunted even his detractors, and his predictions were nothing if not dour. One day, while walking across a large field in Drummossie, he supposedly fell down and wailed, "This black moor shall be stained with the best blood in the Highlands. Heads will be lopped off by the score, and no mercy will be shown or quarter given on either side." He was kneeling on Culloden Moor, the future site of the terrible massacre of the Scots during the rebellion of 1745-46.

Word of his uncanny success is said to have elevated Odhar from a local curiosity to a man of great renown and status. He began to predict the future, charging high fees to rich families on the Scottish mainland. For all his apparent powers, however, Odhar's vanity may have prevented him from predicting his own demise. One day at the height of his fame, he was summoned to Brahan Castle, near Dingwall, by Isabella, the wife of the third earl of Seaforth. The earl was long overdue from a journey to Paris, and the countess was beside herself with worry. She begged Odhar to use his powers to alleviate her fears.

According to the story, the seer gazed through his stone and then broke into a lewd grin. "Madam," he said, "there is no need to worry concerning your husband's welfare. He is well and merry." Isabella pressed for more details, which he refused to give. Finally, when she resorted to threats, he snapped back that in his vision he had seen the earl in a sumptuous Parisian salon with his arms around another woman.

After a moment of silence, the countess spoke. "You have sullied the good name of my lord in the halls of his ancestors, and you shall suffer the most signal vengeance I can inflict"—death on the pyre. The earl returned from Paris as Odhar was being taken to be burned alive. Upon hearing the news, and knowing Odhar's words to be true, he rode off to stay the execution.

Meanwhile, Odhar, who had been sure that the countess would, upon reflection, reduce the initial sentence, at last realized that she was determined to carry out her threat. In fear and rage he is said to have cried out the final prophecy that earned him the title of the Brahan Seer: "I see in the far future the doom of the race of my oppressor. I see a chief, the last of his house, both deaf and dumb. He will be the father of four sons, all of whom he will follow to the tomb. The remnant of his possessions shall be inherited by a white-coifed lassie from the East, and she is to kill her sister." Isabella was so incensed by this that she ordered her men to carry out the execution by thrusting Odhar headfirst into a barrel lined with sharp stakes and filled with burning tar. The earl was too late to halt this grisly deed. A few years afterward, Isabella threw herself out of the castle tower to her death.

One by one, each element of Odhar's reputed dying prophecy came to pass. An earl of Seaforth born in 1754 lost his hearing to scarlet fever when he was about twelve. Each of his four sons died young, and after those tragedies, he also lost his power of speech. He died on January 11, 1815, and one of his daughters returned to Scotland not long afterward from her home in India, where her husband had recently died; she was dressed in traditional white mourning clothes. The woman eventually remarried, and since there were no male heirs, the Seaforth lands passed to her and her second husband. One day, the carriage she was driving overturned and killed her sister, thus concluding the last act of the predicted tragedy.

Many of Odhar's alleged prophecies came true years after his death. He supposedly predicted that the eight-ton Stone of Petty, situated well inland, would end up in the sea—as it did, after a hurricane in 1799 struck the area and apparently dislodged the stone. And there are those who maintain that one legendary prediction may yet come to pass. Coinneach Odhar is said to have foretold that "a dun hornless cow will appear in Minch and will make a bellow which will knock the six chimneys off Gairloch House. The whole country will become utterly desolated, after which deer and other wild animals shall be exterminated by horrid black rain." Some doomsayers see the dun hornless cow as a nuclear submarine and the bellow as a nuclear explosion with its consequent devastation and fallout. Intriguingly enough, Gairloch House had no chimneys at the time of this prophecy; today it has six.

One thing missing from the Brahan Seer tales is a detailed discussion of Odhar's mystical blue stone. But if it fit the pattern of other time-honored tools of divination, the scrying stone was not so much a magic talisman as it was a device that allowed a powerful intellect to focus its concentration. Nature supplied humankind's first symbols of hidden knowledge—stones, water, flowers, birds, clouds—and in seeking to divine messages from them, our ancestors may have taken their earliest steps down the road to the sciences of biology, geology, and even meteorology.

In the modern world, reading tea leaves and gazing into crystal balls are two of the more familiar methods of natural divination, but there are many other traditional techniques, each with its own title ending in "mancy," a suffix based on the Greek word *mantis*, meaning "diviner" or "prophet." Capnomancy is the practice of reading portents in the way rising smoke drifts in the wind; apantomancy explores the significance of meeting animals—giving rise, for example, to the notion that if a black cat crosses your path, bad luck is on its way. Anthropomancy, perhaps the darkest art of all, is divination through human sacrifice. Happily, most forms of natural divination seem more bizarre than sinister.

Divination from nature may be rooted in ancient shamanic rituals. For at least 25,000 years, shamans have played their part as priests, magicians, and healers. Portraits of entranced shamans decorate the walls of Stone Age caves; even today, in parts of Asia, the Arctic, and the Americas, these supposed magicians practice their arts.

This bronze model of a sheep's liver served as a guide for ancient Etruscans learning the complex art of hepatoscopy, or "liver gazing." Each of the model's forty segments, as well as the raised areas, is associated with a different god or element of nature.

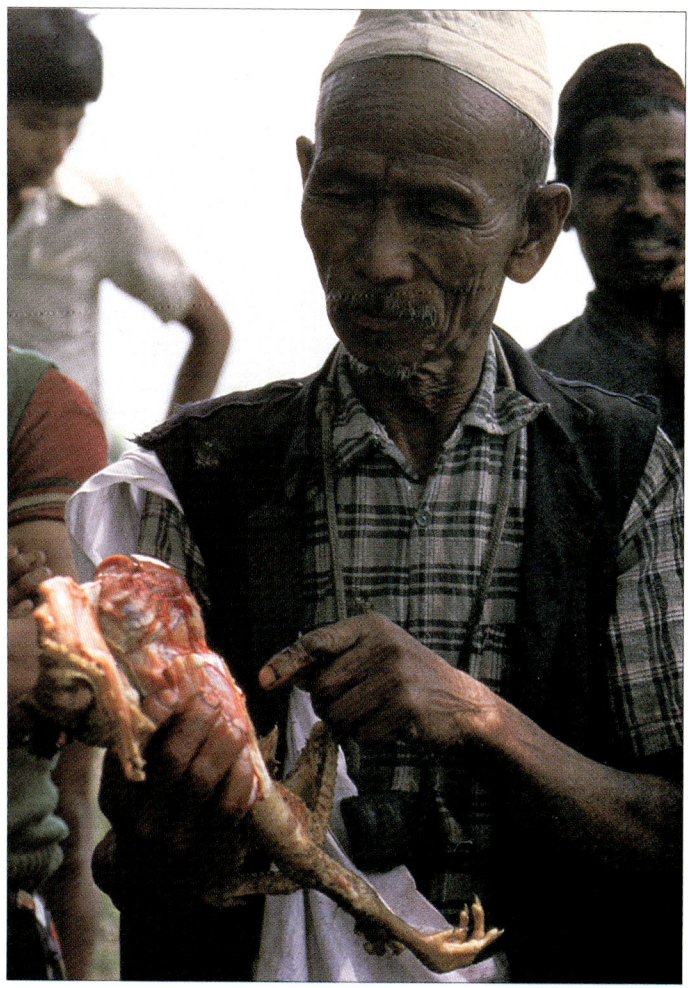

Practicing the somewhat grisly method of prophecy known as haruspicy, a Gurung shaman examines the innards of a sacrificed chicken. For the Gurung, a farming people living in Nepal, the shape and color of the bird's lungs may foretell sickness or good fortune.

Central to shamanic belief is the idea that a sacred living spirit inhabits all of the natural world, even the stones. Shamans undergo intense physical trials to gain an understanding of this force, an understanding that is said to enable them to discern the future. As one modern Siberian Chukchee shaman has said: "On the steep bank of a river, there exists life. A voice is there and speaks aloud. I saw the master of the voice and spoke with him. He subjugated himself to me and sacrificed to me. He came yesterday and answered my questions. The small gray bird with the blue breast comes to me and sings shaman songs in the hollow of the bough, calls her spirits, and practices shamanism."

As Western cultures developed and codified such techniques, divination became more formal. The early Greeks and Romans, for instance, assumed that almost every natural event was a sign from the gods. Hence any unusual happening, from a hailstorm to the birth of a deformed calf, was deemed an urgent message from on high.

To be sure, there was frequent evidence of the fallibility of divination. In one notable example, the Athenian general Nicias was seeking in 413 BC to capture Syracuse in a sea battle, only to be thwarted by the city's brave defenders. On the night the Greek ships were poised to retreat, the full moon that would have guided them home was extinguished by an eclipse. The sailors panicked. Nicias summoned a diviner, but since his usual seer had recently died, he had to rely on an unseasoned substitute who explained the eclipse as a directive from the gods to delay the retreat for twenty-seven days, or one cycle of the moon. Accepting his judgment, the Athenians remained, only to be crushed by the vengeful Syracusans. Twenty-seven thousand soldiers died, and the remaining 13,000 ended their lives in slavery. Nicias was killed and his body displayed on the city wall.

In ancient Rome, divination split into several distinct functions. Chief among these was augury. Regarded at the time as a profound science, augury was the study of eclipses as well as of thunder, the behavior of birds and animals, and other natural signs, called auspices. Augurs sought divine approval for the decisions and actions of society's leaders. Since elections, consecrations, and declarations of war could be held in abeyance until they were augured auspicious, these seers exerted enormous control over the lives of citizens and the fates of the communities.

Augurs in early Rome adopted many of their practices from the older Etruscan culture, passing their intricate system orally from generation to generation. As time went by, augury became institutionalized in the Roman Republic, and augurs were gathered into a formal college, along with the pontiffs, who administered public ceremonies, and the keepers of the Sibylline books (a collection of ancient oracular prophecies). The augurs' readings were recorded and stored, with the subsequent outcomes, in secret archives.

To take important auspices, the blindfolded augur would go with a magistrate to some outdoor setting. The official would then survey the land and sky and tell the augur what he saw, while the augur explained its meaning. To Roman augurs, lightning was considered a direct communication from Jupiter, the father of all gods, and lightning bolts were interpreted according to the sector of the sky from which they struck. Bolts from the east were good, those from the west were bad, and those from the north

A comet is said to have warned Montezuma of impending danger shortly before the coming of Hernán Cortés in 1519, as depicted in this sixteenth-century illustration. Called smoking stars by the Aztecs, such celestial fireworks were considered the gravest of portents, often seen as omens of doom.

were the most portentous. Hence, northwestern lightning, meaning especially bad news, was greatly feared. Occasionally, though, the message was more direct. A bolt is said to have struck a statue of Caesar Augustus, actually melting the first letter of the word *Caesar*. Since the letter C was the Roman numeral for 100, his augurs predicted that he would live only 100 more days—as he supposedly did.

In another form of Roman augury, alectryomancers kept their eyes on common roosters. These augurs drew a circle in the dirt and divided it into pie segments with a letter of the alphabet in each one. After they scattered feed on this emblem, the rooster ate his way around the circle; the order of the lettered segments from which it took the grain spelled out the answers to augurs' questions.

Perhaps the most elaborate form of classical divination was the inspection of the entrails of sacrificed animals for signs of the gods' wishes. Called haruspicy, this practice came to the Greeks and Romans from either the Etruscans or the earlier cultures of Babylonia and Assyria. Its underlying theory was that when an animal—usually a sheep or an ox—was sacrificed, it was absorbed by the god to which it had been offered, creating a direct channel to the deity. By

> ## 44 Ways of Looking Ahead
>
> Over the centuries an astonishing variety of natural objects and occurrences have been used as means of divining the future. The sampling below provides an overview of some of the most common—and more curious—modes of prophecy.
>
> **Aeromancy**—by the observation of atmospheric phenomena.
> **Alphitomancy**—by the swallowing of a specially baked barley loaf.
> **Axinomancy**—by a stone balanced on a red-hot ax.
> **Austromancy**—by the study of winds.
> **Botanomancy**—by the burning of briar or vervain branches.
> **Cephalomancy**—by boiling a donkey's head.
> **Ceromancy**—by the observation of the shapes formed by dripping melted wax into water.
> **Chalcomancy**—by interpreting the tones made by striking copper or brass bowls.
> **Chresmomancy**—by the utterances of a person in a frenzy.
> **Cromniomancy**—by observing the growth of specially prepared onions.
> **Daphnomancy**—by the sound of burning laurel leaves.
> **Felidomancy**—by the behavior and actions of cats.
> **Floromancy**—by the study of flowers or plants.
> **Gelomancy**—by the interpretation of hysterical laughter.
> **Gyromancy**—by the mutterings of those exhausted by wild dancing.
> **Halomancy**—by casting salt into fire.
> **Hippomancy**—by observing the gait of horses during ceremonial processions.
> **Ichthyomancy**—by the examination of fish, living or dead.
> **Lithomancy**—by the reflection of candlelight in precious stones.
> **Lychnomancy**—by watching flames of three candles forming a triangle.
> **Macharomancy**—by swords, daggers, and knives.
> **Margaritomancy**—by the action of a charmed pearl in a covered pot.
> **Metopomancy or Metoposcopy**—by the lines on a person's forehead.
> **Myomancy**—by the sounds, actions, or sudden appearance of rats or mice.
> **Nephelomancy**—by the movement and shape of clouds.
> **Oenomancy**—by the color, appearance, and taste of wines.
> **Omphalomancy**—by contemplation of one's own navel.
> **Oneiromancy**—by the interpretation of dreams and night visions.
> **Onychomancy**—by the reflection of sunlight on fingernails.
> **Ophiomancy**—by the study of serpents.
> **Ovomancy**—by observing the shapes formed by dropping egg whites into water.
> **Phyllorhodomancy**—by the sounds of rose leaves clapped against the hands.
> **Podomancy**—by study of the soles of the feet.
> **Scapulomancy**—by the markings on the shoulder bone of an animal.
> **Sciomancy**—by the size, shape, and changing appearance of shadows of the dead.
> **Selenomancy**—by the phases and appearances of the moon.
> **Sideromancy**—by the shapes formed by dropping dry straw onto a hot iron.
> **Splanchomancy**—by examining the entrails of sacrificial victims.
> **Sycomancy**—by the drying of fig leaves.
> **Transataumancy**—by events seen or heard accidentally.
> **Tyromancy**—by the coagulation of cheese.
> **Uromancy**—by inspection of urine.
> **Xylomancy**—by interpreting the appearance of fallen tree branches or observing the positions of burning logs.
> **Zoomancy**—by reports of imaginary animals, such as sea monsters.

opening the carcass, the haruspex presumed to peek inside the god's mind and watch the future being created.

Their assumptions may have been dubious, but if nothing else, ancient haruspices learned anatomy. In Babylonian and Etruscan ruins, archaeologists have discovered remarkably accurate models of livers, covered with inscriptions pertaining to gods and the heavens. Apparently, haruspices were particularly interested in the *processus pyramidalis,* the liver's pyramid-shaped projection. A large one was taken as a sign of good tidings, but a cleft one meant disruptions ahead. Indeed, several days before March 15, 44 BC, Spurinna Vestricius, Julius Caesar's haruspex, discovered that the liver of a sacrificed bull had no processus pyramidalis at all and warned his patron to watch out for his life. Caesar ignored this timely advice and died as predicted on the infamous Ides of March, of twenty-three dagger wounds inflicted by a group of his closest associates.

In time, haruspices succeeded augurs as the leading official government diviners, but eventually both practices degenerated into superstition, commercialism, and outright fraud. In one instance, a Greek haruspex named Soudinos, to encourage an army that was going into battle, inked the phrase "victory of the king" in reverse on his palm. When he lifted the liver out of its carcass, this war cry was "miraculously" on the organ, spurring the soldiers to battle. Whether they were indeed victorious is not recorded.

Outside the centers of Mediterranean culture, less-civilized peoples practiced their own forms of divination. In stark contrast to the Greeks and Romans, who generally conducted their elaborate rituals in glistening marble temples, the Druids of northern Europe celebrated their mysteries deep in the primeval forests. In the darkling shade of spreading oaks, novices were initiated into Druidical orders by tutelage that lasted as long as twenty years.

The Druids were the spiritual leaders of the Celts, a people who, before the Roman conquests, could be found in Spain, France, Germany, Britain, and as far east as Poland and Turkey. Celts often claimed an inherited characteristic they called *an-da-sheal-ladh*, "the two sights," but its mature exercise was a privilege reserved for Druids.

What little we know of this select class comes largely from classical authors. Druids formed a Celtic priesthood, responsible for passing along traditional lore, administering justice, overseeing religious ceremonies, and performing divinations. But the Romans looked upon the priests as primitive and abhorrent, particularly when they discovered that Druidical methods of divination included human sacrifice. In peacetime, the Druids sacrificed pairs of white bulls, but when at war, they dispatched captured enemies or criminals. The hapless "offerings" were confined within gigantic wicker sculptures, which were then burned. As the flames mounted, the priests would calmly practice their pyromancy and anthropomancy, reading the future in the smoke and flames and in the screams of their victims.

As the Romans conquered more of the Celtic domain, they tried to wipe out such practices. Later, Christian missionaries continued the effort, even ordering the wholesale slaughter of wrens, birds prized by the Celts because their twitterings were thought to contain prophecies.

But the old ways may not have been completely crushed by the military might of the Romans and the weight of Christianity. Some believe the most famous of all magicians, Merlin of the King Arthur legend, may have been a Druid who practiced as late as AD 500. Even today, members of an English cult claiming Druid ancestry perform ancient rituals during the summer solstice at Stonehenge, erroneously thought by some to have been built by Druids as a ceremonial center.

Druids and augurs may no longer play an important role in society, but their divinatory advice lives on, especially in folk beliefs about the significance of weather, plant, and animal omens. Four-leaf clovers continue to represent good luck, and a stork flying over a house is still supposed by some to proclaim an imminent pregnancy.

Ancient legends recount how those who ignored the wisdom of animals did so at their peril. On the eve of a sea

On a Mexico City street corner, Lucerito the Trained
Canary selects at random a card that will reveal the fortune of a passerby
who has paid a few pesos to the bird's owner.

battle with the Carthaginians, Claudius Pulcher, a headstrong Roman naval commander, chose to ignore a rather pointed animal omen: The sacred chickens on his ship stopped eating. "Throw the damn chickens into the sea!" he shouted. "If they won't eat, let them drink!" The Roman sailors followed their leader's bidding and were badly beaten by the Carthaginians.

Long after formalized augury died out, the behavior of birds interested omen watchers. In England, for instance, ravens still have special significance. A family of them has occupied the Tower of London for centuries, and it is generally supposed that if they ever fly off, the royal family will die out. By the same token, it is said that Britain's dominion over the fortress of Gibraltar will end if the native population of Barbary apes deserts the rocky peninsula.

Many people still believe animals to be prescient and their actions full of divinatory significance. Such beliefs may be fostered by the fact that many animals have far greater powers of sight, hearing, and smell than humans do. Dogs, for example, are supposed to be able to predict the death of their masters, but perhaps they are merely detecting subtle chemical changes in the body; it may be that the supposed psychic power of these loyal pets is nothing more than a keen sense of smell.

Even insects are said to have powers of foresight. The clicking of the so-called deathwatch beetle was once believed to foretell death in the home it infested. This alleged harbinger was taken quite seriously in the eighteenth century. As the Englishman Duncan Campbell wrote scornfully in 1732, "How many people have I seen in the most terrible palpitations, for months together, expecting every hour the approach of some calamity, only by a little worm which breeds in an old wainscot, and, endeavoring to eat its way out, makes a noise like the movement of a watch."

The art of reading coffee grounds, demonstrated by these Frenchwomen in 1909, is similar to that of reading tea leaves. The sediment is the key; ancient Romans read the dregs of wine.

Ideas about the supposed wisdom of plants have also persisted into modern times. Many people, for example, still believe that laurel thrown on a fire portends good if it crackles and evil if it burns silently—a notion that may be rooted in the days of the Roman Empire, when there was a laurel grove in the capital composed of trees planted by each emperor as he ascended to the throne. But in AD 68, the last year of Emperor Nero's life, the entire grove withered and died, heralding the demise of the line of Caesars.

The use of plants in divination was formalized in the mid-eighteenth century when the Frenchman Rinoir Montaire, a professor at the University of Lyons, devised a briefly popular system known as the Floral Oracle. His clients chose flowers from a large bouquet, their selections supposedly showing underlying characters and future careers. The thistle, not surprisingly, denoted a surly temperament, while a scarlet geranium, for more obscure reasons, revealed stupidity. The subject who picked an apple blossom would become a lawyer; a lily pointed toward politics.

Among the most sought-after forms of divination are those that predict the weather. Even in the technologically advanced twentieth century, accurate weather prediction is important; in previous eras, more affected by the whims of nature, it was a vital skill. Forecasters of old scrutinized everything from the behavior of heavenly bodies to the appetites of fleas for clues to the next day's rain or shine.

On occasion, such predictions threw whole societies into turmoil. In one such case, an almanac published in 1499 by one Johannes Stöffler predicted that a planetary convergence on February 2, 1524, would cause a European reenactment of Noah's flood. As the date approached, as many as 137 pamphlets on the coming disaster were in circulation. The people of Toulouse, France, built and stocked enormous arks. The margrave of Brandenburg, Germany, collected a number of fellow citizens and retreated to the hilltop of Kreuzberg, near Berlin—only to climb down again after it became clear that no flood would occur.

For all of the technology and human energy devoted to it, modern meteorology is still a young and uncertain science. The first barometer, built by Galileo's student Evangelista Torricelli in the seventeenth century, could indicate weather trends for just a day or two in advance, and even today's meteorologists, equipped with many more-sophisticated instruments, will admit that the soundness of their forecasts diminishes to zero for predictions made more than five to ten days in advance.

Given the gap between the desire for perfect weather forecasts and the means to achieve them, it is no surprise that weather folklore has survived through the ages. One time-honored method relies on a calendar of predictions based on saints' days. According to this system, if there is a frost on Saint Sulpicius's day (January 17), it will be a fine spring, whereas if Saint Vincent's day (January 22) is sunny, the following season will be good for wine crops. Also surviving are hundreds of folk sayings based on the behavior of virtually every common animal. "When cockroaches fly, rain will come," claims one adage. "Sharks swim out to sea when a wave of cold weather approaches," says another.

And many Americans still believe that when the wooily caterpillar's brown band is wide, a mild winter lies ahead.

In the words of one weather researcher, most such beliefs "crumple by the weight of their own demerit" when tested. But not all of them are inaccurate. Unlike other forms of divination, which presuppose a certain degree of blind faith, the objective validity of some of these natural indicators has been examined by scientists. Biologists claim that birds do in fact fly closer to the ground before a storm, just as folklore has it. It seems they find the low-pressure air preceding a storm uncomfortable and seek lower altitudes where the pressure is more to their liking.

Indeed, the raw materials of meteorology—temperature, humidity, air pressure, and wind speed—can all be discerned by keen observers of nature without complicated instruments. Mare's tails (wispy cloud trails) usually precede a warm front, while cold fronts are often signaled by a mackerel sky (bunches of puffy, altocumulus clouds).

And Jesus' declaration to the Pharisees, "When it is evening, ye say, it will be fair weather: for the sky is red," is still valid. Actually, the red referred to in many sayings is closer to pink, for pink sunsets signal dry weather ahead, the color being caused by sunlight passing through dust. The light of a blood-red sunset shines through water vapor, a sign of wet weather to come.

ecognizing that such sayings are often accurate, scientists have augmented their earthquake research with serious studies of folklore, including the observation of abnormal animal behavior and other changes in nature as a means of early quake detection. In China, for example, where earthquakes are frequent and often devastating, the government has enlisted as many as 100,000 amateur earthquake watchers, who monitor warning signs such as shifting water levels.

That such traditional signs can be valid indicators of impending seismic upheavals was amply shown in early 1975, when seismologists measuring vibrations within the earth found evidence that a major quake would strike near the port city of Yingkow. At about the same time, local citizens began to witness nature's own indicators: Wells bubbled, rats and mice staggered around in the open as if drugged, and snakes emerged from their winter holes to freeze to death on the surface. On February 4—as anomalous animal behavior increased along with seismic activity—the citizens of Yingkow were evacuated. That evening, a monstrous earthquake demolished the city.

As tempting as it may be to ascribe psychic powers to animals, more mundane explanations may serve. Under certain atmospheric conditions, for example, human beings can hear particularly loud sounds from 600 miles away. An animal with much better hearing than humans may well sense the sound waves of breaking earthquakes while they are still rumbling deep below the earth's crust.

Most people living in earthquake zones would surely feel more confident relying for their warnings on the work of scientists rather than on the antic behavior of snakes, rats, and mice; reliance on natural omens to predict the weather has also waned. At the same time, however, divination through observing natural occurrences has evolved into more symbolic forms, involving the supposedly psychic powers of the human mind.

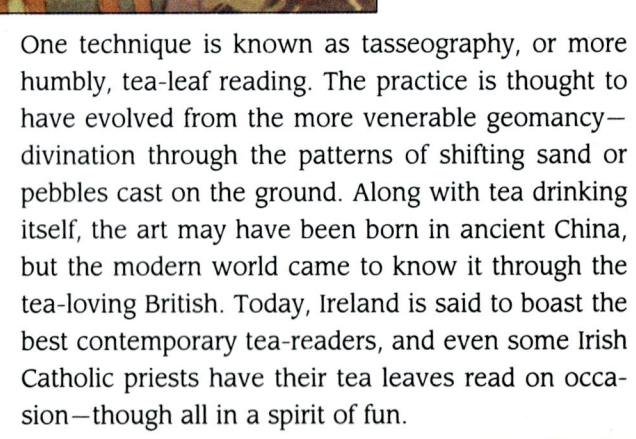

One technique is known as tasseography, or more humbly, tea-leaf reading. The practice is thought to have evolved from the more venerable geomancy—divination through the patterns of shifting sand or pebbles cast on the ground. Along with tea drinking itself, the art may have been born in ancient China, but the modern world came to know it through the tea-loving British. Today, Ireland is said to boast the best contemporary tea-readers, and even some Irish Catholic priests have their tea leaves read on occasion—though all in a spirit of fun.

In the United States, tasseography is often practiced in the ubiquitous Gypsy tearooms of larger cities, where a hostess provides an indifferent meal and a cup of tea before performing a reading. These shamelessly commercial establishments have given tea-leaf reading a tawdry reputation. For example, the reputed psychic Eileen Garrett, who remained skeptical about most forms of fortune-telling, recounted in one of her books the tale of a lonely country schoolteacher who came to New York in the early part of

Rearing horses, panicked pigs and fowl, and leaping fish may be harbingers of an earthquake, according to four scenes taken from a modern Chinese educational poster (opposite). Scientists there take heed of these and other natural omens, such as irregularities in well water (above), to help anticipate and prepare for major tremors.

this century and had her tea leaves read. During the sitting, the reader picked up clues that her client held a secret passion for her happily married local minister. Playing on the teacher's hidden desires, the reader hinted that the leaves indicated the minister's wife was engaged in an extramarital affair. This information apparently goaded the teacher into sending anonymous warning notes to the minister, thereby causing a great scandal. Eventually she was driven to confess what she had done and was forced to leave both her job and her community.

To be sure, would-be subjects of a tasseography session can avoid the risk of being thus manipulated by reading their own tea leaves. In a recent book on the subject, seasoned leaf reader Ian McKinnie—who practices his art in Santa Rosa, California—explained the technique. He recommends starting with the right sort of tea: English breakfast—loose tea, not tea bags. (In a pinch, coffee grounds can be substituted for tea leaves.) Brew the tea and pour it with some of the leaves into a plain bone-china cup. After drinking all but the last half-teaspoonful, swirl the cup around several times and turn it upside down into its saucer. Wait a few moments for the liquid to drain out, then lift the cup, turn it over, and examine the pattern of leaves that should be clinging to the interior.

Look for the shapes of familiar images in the scattered leaves. Said to portend future events, the more obvious ones include an airplane (an imminent journey), an angel (good tidings), a beehive (prosperity), and a mountain (either an obstacle or great ambition). Some of the more obscure images are opera glasses (a quarrel), a kangaroo (domestic harmony), a saucepan (anxiety), and a steeple (a setback). Mice or rats mean danger or bad financial news, which grows worse with the length of their tails.

In addition to displaying such portents, McKinnie believes, the distribution of the leaves within the cup says something about the seeker's personality. Leaves spread evenly all around the cup denote an outgoing optimist; one large clump at the bottom indicates a stick-in-the-mud.

McKinnie claims much success in his tasseographical career. In one case, he says, the leaves enabled him to predict that a high-school friend of his daughter would become a flight attendant, marry her current boyfriend, and move to Australia—all three of which she eventually did.

Because its perceived omens are so subjective, tas-

*In 1935 a vision in the sacred lake of Lhamo Latso
reportedly guided a Tibetan council to their new spiritual ruler; the fourteenth
Dalai Lama (right) was only two years old at the time.*

seography is most often—and perhaps most appropriately—treated as entertainment rather than a serious attempt at divination. As a dubious Eileen Garrett once put it: "Have you ever really *looked* at wet tea leaves? . . . I must confess that to my jaundiced eye, they reveal very little . . . . What astute jurisdiction is to decide whether that wiggly line of leaves is a snake, the symbol of evil, or a serpentine line, the symbol of fortune? . . . To get any picture out of them at all requires a most abundantly fertile imagination."

Possibly the most pervasive form of natural divination is known as scrying, in which a practitioner presumes to plumb the depths of hidden knowledge by concentrating on a smooth, clear, or reflective surface. Derived from the old word *descry*, meaning to catch sight of, scrying takes many forms. Ancient Greeks practiced hydromancy, or scrying in the waters of a spring, such as the one in front of the goddess Demeter's sanctuary. To see the fate of a sick person, hydromancers lowered a mirror on a string to the water's surface, letting it graze the water. When they pulled the mirror back up and looked at it, they supposedly would see the image of the person as either dead or living.

Gastromancy was another form of scrying. According to the sixth-century philosopher Damascius, gastromancers "filled certain round glasses with fair water, about which they placed lighted torches, then invoked the question to be solved. At length, the demon answered by reflections from the water representing what should come to pass."

In ancient India, warriors often practiced cylicomancy, peering into a vessel of water before heading into battle. If they saw their reflections, they knew they would return. Tahitians claimed to use cylicomancy to track down robbers. After digging a hole in the earthen floor of a burglarized house, the cylicomancer would fill the space with water, pray to a deity, and wait for the image of the culprit to be revealed on the surface of the water.

Despite—or perhaps because of—scrying's widespread acceptance in ancient times, early Christian leaders were dead set against it. Saint Patrick declared that any Christians who believed demons could be seen in mirrors would be expelled from the Church until they repented. Even so, the Middle Ages continued to foster scrying of all sorts, and scryers used every aid from fingernails to swords.

Roger Bacon, the thirteenth-century British scholar and mystic, was reported to possess a glass "of excellent nature, that any man might beholde any thing that he desired to see, within the compass of fifty miles round about him." (Some historians now believe that this legend may have grown out of Bacon's studies of optics.) Later in his life, however, Bacon was imprisoned for some of his occult practices, as well as for his attacks on established theologians and scholars of the time. And in 1467, when one William Byg of Yorkshire confessed that he had used a crystal in order to find his neighbors' stolen property, he was forced to march to the Cathedral of Saint Peter at York, recant, and burn his books.

Virtually every kind of smooth or reflective object has been used for scrying, including the simple stone of Coinneach Odhar, the Brahan Seer. Others have claimed to use the back of a watch, a door lock, an eggshell, and soap bubbles. One contemporary scryer says he has employed a blank television screen, a radiator, the outside of a black coffee cup, and even his own highly polished shoes.

For sheer potency, however, no scrying tool outdoes the alleged powers of the familiar yet enigmatic crystal ball. And no crystal gazer has cut a more dramatic swath through history than the Englishman John Dee—mathematician, philosopher, and adviser to Queen Elizabeth I.

The son of a minor palace official in the court of Henry VIII, Dee was an exceptional student who entered Cambridge University when he was fifteen. Although he claimed to study a full eighteen hours a day, Dee once took time out to build an intricate prop for a school play: a high-flying beetle that carried the hero of a Greek drama up to the ceiling. The audience was reputedly so terrified by the spectacle that a number of them jumped up during the performance shouting, "Sorcerer!"

ee excelled at Cambridge and was named Underreader (junior faculty member) before taking his degree. After graduating he traveled to the Continent to continue his studies, achieving overnight fame in Paris at the age of twenty-three, when he delivered a series of lectures on the recently exhumed works of the Greek mathematician Euclid. Like other classical sciences, mathematics had languished in Europe during the Middle Ages, and it continued to possess an air of magic and forbidden knowledge in the sixteenth century. Dee's lectures caused a sensation, and thousands of students packed the lecture hall and scaled the outside walls in order to listen to them.

After returning to England in 1551, Dee met the future Queen Elizabeth while she was being held under house arrest by Queen Mary. The two developed a friendship that lasted for the rest of their lives. As queen, Elizabeth gave Dee money and eventually a royal assignment as warden of Christ's College in Manchester. More importantly, she protected him from those who accused him of witchcraft. She even set the date for her coronation in 1558 according to his astrological calculations.

Dee's house in Mortlake, near London, was for many years a major center of science in England. Dee salvaged many ancient scientific tomes that had been scattered when Roman Catholic churches and monasteries were ransacked during the Reformation, and his own library of more than 4,000 books may have been the largest of its kind in Europe at the time.

In the year 1581, however, John Dee's life swerved onto an entirely new path. He later wrote of how, as he knelt in prayer late one autumn evening, "there suddenly glowed a dazzling light, in the midst of which, in all his glory, stood the great angel, Uriel." The spirit reportedly handed Dee a crystal "most bright, most clear and glorious, of the bigness of an egg" and informed him that by gazing at it he could communicate with otherworldly spirits. John Dee was enraptured by this prospect, but in spite of the angel's promise, he had little luck at scrying with this "shew-stone." The scientist resorted to employing others to do the actual scrying, conversing directly with the spirits, while he kept scrupulous notes.

Unfortunately Dee's scryers were less scrupulous than he. The one with him the longest was Edward Kelley. A classic Renaissance scoundrel, Kelley was an erstwhile lawyer who had already had his ears cropped for counterfeiting before he met Dee. He also stood accused of necromancy—the practice of using dead bodies for divination.

Kelley was unquestionably a charlatan, but his attempts at scrying with Dee may well have been honest—at least at the beginning. Gazing into the glass, he reported to Dee that "in the middle of the stone seemeth to stand a little round thing like a spark of fire, and it increaseth, and it seemeth to be as a globe of twenty inches diameter, or there about." In this glowing central sphere, Kelley claimed to raise a host of spiritual beings who attempted, among other things, to teach Dee "Enochian," the language spoken by angels and the inhabitants of the Garden of Eden. In fact, Dee's alleged Enochian records are elaborate enough to have convinced some credulous readers that they represented a genuine pre-Hebraic language. But at least one researcher has suggested that Enochian was a code Dee used to transmit messages from overseas to Queen Elizabeth in his alleged capacity as a founding member of the English secret service.

Dee's avid interest in crystallomancy seems to have been merely part of his driving intellectual quest to understand the secrets of the natural world. To his restless mind, there was no distinction between magic and science—knowledge was knowledge, and who better than angels to provide it? The sly Kelley, on the other hand, was more interested in acquiring instant wealth through alchemy, espe-

Catherine de Médicis watches in wonder as, in this idealized 1887 engraving, the famed prophet Nostradamus causes the royal destinies of her sons to appear in a mirror. The Queen of France regularly consulted the seer, who probably censored his forecasts to suit her expectations.

cially by way of the long-sought secret of transforming base metal into gold. In pursuit of both ideals, Dee and Kelley eventually made their way to Poland in 1583 at the request of Count Albert Laski, who hoped they would help him master the alchemical sciences.

By this time, Edward Kelley seemed to have Dee firmly under his control, but one day he finally took things too far. On April 18, 1587, he announced that the crystal had ordered the pair to share their wives. So dependent was Dee on Kelley that he and his wife actually signed an agreement to do so. Whether the pact was ever consummated is unclear, but soon afterward the Dees returned—without Kelley—to England.

The irrepressible Kelley then moved on to Prague at the invitation of Holy Roman Emperor Rudolf II, who also hoped to learn the secret of alchemy. When Kelley failed to provide it, he was thrown into prison on charges of sorcery and fraud. In 1593 he tried to escape by climbing down from a high window, but his improvised ladder of bedsheets gave way under his considerable bulk, and he fell, breaking many bones. He died the next day.

Dee's fortunes were not much better. His patron Elizabeth died in 1603. He tried two other scryers, both dishonest, and finally ended up, in the words of the biographer John Aubrey, as a beaten old man with "a long beard as white as milke, tall and slender, who wore a gowne with hanging sleeves." He earned a pittance telling fortunes and even sold his beloved books, one by one, in order to eat. Dee died in 1608, his dreams of sublime knowledge long since dashed. He did, however, gain a measure of immortal-

20

The smoky-quartz globe at left was one of a number of crystal balls used by the sixteenth-century English scientist and astrologer John Dee. Dee relied on others, most notably the unscrupulous Edward Kelley, to do his viewing. It was Kelley who allegedly saw a vision instructing Dee to prepare a wax talisman upon which to rest his crystal ball (left, bottom); carved into the wax were a cross and other sacred markings apparently intended to ward off evil spirits.

ity: Some believe he may have served as the model for Shakespeare's Prospero, the learned sorcerer of *The Tempest.*

Among all the means of scrying, crystallomancy has continued to hold center stage. And like so many other forms of the occult, it flourished in the late-nineteenth-century heyday of spiritualism. One of the more colorful crystal gazers of that era was Nell St. John Montague, an Englishwoman whose autobiography, *Revelations of a Society Clairvoyante,* shows a flair for the thrilling tale.

Montague was born in India not long before the turn of the century, the daughter of Major General C. B. Lucie-Smith. Her favorite childhood toy, she wrote, was a crystal ball given to her by her Indian nurse. One day when she was about five years old, Montague related, she was gazing into the ball when it suddenly seemed to move and become shapeless. "In its place," according to Montague, "came a thick black mist which seemed to spread, enveloping all the space before me. Then slowly in the blackness I saw reflected the interior of my mother's bedroom, and my eyes became focused upon the blue embroidered dressing-gown laid on the bed ready for her to put on. . . . My mother was approaching the bed, her hands outstretched to pick the garment up, when, almost paralysed with horror, I saw something uncoil itself from amongst the soft silkfolds. A wild shriek broke from me, and I dropped the ball, as the concealed cobra darted out and reared to strike."

The terrified young girl ran for comfort to her mother, who assumed that her child's screams resulted from a nightmare. Hoping to ease her fears, Mrs. Lucie-Smith summoned a sentry, and the three went to the bedroom to investigate. As Montague told the story, her mother told her to look and assure herself that there was no snake in the room. "Then to show the truth of her words she approached the bed. As she did so, a loud cry broke from the sentry's lips, and with wonderful courage he pushed her aside and sprang forward, his bayonet uplifted to strike the cobra which had suddenly darted out, and reared up with inflated hood."

From then on, according to Montague, her parents believed firmly in her powers, and she went on to a lifetime of successful scrying in Europe. Once, she claimed, while giving a reading for a naval officer, she peered into her crystal and saw several blood-spattered women, their clothes ripped from their bodies. Fearing that her client was or would be a murderer, she nonetheless told him of her vision. About a year later, he wrote to inform her that the vision had come true, that the women were in fact earthquake victims from Messina, Italy, taken aboard his vessel in a rescue effort. On another occasion, an Englishwoman living in India wrote and asked for a reading, enclosing a letter from her young son. Montague placed the letter against her crystal ball and saw an image of three boys being mistreated by a "vile-looking" clergyman. Informed of the vision, the woman expressed some surprise, noting that her son, a student at an English boarding school, had described in his letters the warm, loving care he was receiving. Not long afterward, according to Montague's account, she herself discovered the boarding school—conveniently located next door to a good friend of hers—and liberated the boy from the clutches of the abusive headmaster. Montague continued her readings until she was killed in a World War II London air raid—presumably having failed to foresee her violent end.

Nell Montague and other scryers of her era inspired many amateurs, who were further encouraged when the renowned English psychic researcher Frederic W. H. Myers estimated in the late 1800s that one in twenty people had scrying abilities. And a number of books published at the time drew on traditional sources to describe the proper techniques for those who wished to try crystal gazing.

The tract *Crystal Gazing and Clairvoyance*, published in 1896 by John Melville, prescribed an elaborate scrying ritual that required equally elaborate paraphernalia—including an ivory or ebony stand for the ball, inlaid with magic words in raised golden letters. In proper Victorian fashion, Melville insisted that the scryer must consecrate all of the implements and repeat a long and pious Christian invocation. He also issued a stern warning to any scryer with evil intentions: "When he or she uses the crystal . . . it will *react* upon the seer sooner or later *with terrible effect.*"

Modern-day scryers are less formal and less fearful than Melville, but their recommendations for successful scrying are still complex. According to one author, the ball should be round or oval and about four inches in diameter. A natural crystal is preferred, although glass is less expensive and perfectly acceptable.

Ideally, the orb should be kept in the dark and always in the same place, to avoid extreme temperature changes and unwanted influences. It must also be spotless and unscratched so that imperfections will not distract the scryer. One age-old cleaning technique calls for boiling it in a five-to-one mixture of water and brandy for fifteen minutes and then drying it with a chamois cloth. For a few days before scrying, says another author, one should also purify one's thoughts through positive thinking, one's body through frequent baths, and one's insides by a judicious diet.

A dimly lit room is ideal for the reading. The orb should be surrounded by dark, heavy cloth—such as velvet—to cut down on distracting reflections, and it should be viewed from about a foot away. Some scryers recommend passing one's hands over the ball to increase its power and sensitivity. Others suggest trying to look at the crystal and through it at the same time in order to temporarily short-circuit normal eyesight and induce so-called inner vision.

Within about five minutes, if the scryer is successful, the ball will supposedly become opaque and milky, as if clouds are passing through it. When the clouds disperse, images may form. They might appear as a single static image, in a series like a slide show, or as a full-blown movie-like presentation.

If no images are forthcoming, one might be able to read portents in the clouds alone. According to Melville, whose interpretations are still widely accepted, white ones mean yes or good tidings, while black are, of course, bad news. Bright colors like red and yellow signal unpleasant surprises, while blue and green portend coming joy.

The solid images that appear in a crystal ball are said to be more difficult to interpret objectively, because they have different meanings for each person. Thus an airplane could mean either an impending journey or an unconscious desire to get away from an uncomfortable situation.

Most scryers emphasize that the ball acts not as a telescope into the unknown but as a means of focusing their attention and sharpening innate ability. As Miss Angus, a scryer of the late 1800s, explained, "The moment the *vision* comes the *ball* seems to disappear, so it is difficult for me to say if my pictures are actually seen *in* the crystal."

The Message of the Pendulum

The ancient practice of divining with pendulums is enjoying new popularity. Some modern mystics believe that the swinging motion of a pendant responding to gravity—and perhaps to more mysterious forces as well—can reveal inner truths and foretell the future.

A pendulum is any object suspended so that it can move freely. The weight itself, called a bob, may be made of almost anything. But some pendulum enthusiasts prefer using a quartz crystal, such as the one shown here, in the belief that crystals are keys to unlocking psychic potential.

To make a pendulum, simply attach a weight to a thread, string, or lightweight chain. There are no specific requirements for the thread's length or the bob's weight, but the pendulum should swing easily and be comfortable to hold.

Specialists claim numerous uses for pendulums. The objects purportedly can help diagnose disease, for instance, or help locate water, treasure, or even missing persons. For more general divination, however, the easiest and most widely practiced way to use a pendulum is this: Hold it perfectly still and concentrate on a question that can be answered yes or no. Theoretically the pendulum should move in response, prompted by some mysterious source of truth. The most common interpretation of its message is that rotation in a clockwise direction means yes, a counterclockwise motion no.

The experimenter should know that the slightest movement at the top of the string will be greatly magnified by the bob. Critics observe that pendulum power might therefore be no more than the amplification of the holder's own muscular movement. In other words, a subconscious hope for a particular answer may prompt the slightest inadvertent twitch, which will, in turn, deliver the desired response.

While occultists would argue that the crystal somehow helps its users harness paranormal powers, psychological theory offers another explanation for scrying, suggesting that it is a form of retrieving and projecting knowledge buried in the subconscious. The following experience, related by the English psychical researcher and scryer Ada Goodrich-Freer, seems to support this notion. "The crystal had nothing more attractive to show me than the combination 7694," she wrote of one of her sessions. "I laid aside the crystal and took up my banking-book, which I had certainly not seen for some months, and found, to my surprise, that the number on the cover was 7694."

In a somewhat similar vein, a number of children and some adults exhibit a capacity called eidetic imagery—the ability to stare at an object or scene and then mentally project it onto a wall or other suitable screen. This could account for the fact that in ancient cultures young children were often used as scryers. The images they saw in the mirror or the water may have been projections of images in their memories or imaginations.

In recent years, crystals and other stones have gained a considerable reputation as mystical objects, allegedly useful for healing and meditation as well as divination. Ursula Markham, a British medium, developed her own system of "gemology," employing many semiprecious stones instead of a single crystal orb.

For divination, Markham suggests collecting a wide variety of stones, at least forty. These include labradorite, signifying a place overseas; iron pyrite, or fool's gold, signifying mistrust or deception; purple agate, emblem of emotional sensitivity; green jasper, for unrequited love; and perhaps most important, aquamarine, warning of a cool, logical client who doubts the validity of crystal readings.

For her readings, Markham sits opposite the questioner with her collection of stones in a velvet tray between them. The questioner picks out nine stones, and Markham divines their portent according to the choice and the order in which they were chosen. For example, a tiger's eye (meaning independence) followed by a turritella agate (signifying a change in employment) might indicate that the questioner is thinking of starting a business.

Diviners such as Ursula Markham can rarely provide solid evidence that their techniques actually work. In the final analysis, the efficacy of her stone readings and of tea-leaf readings and scrying must rely on faith: A questioner who believes that a certain form of divination works will be inclined to find evidence that it has. And as Eileen Garrett, a woman who claimed remarkable psychic abilities, once suggested, many diviners and other psychic readers are, if nothing else, at least willing to take the time to listen to their clients, something that physicians, the clergy, and even professional counselors frequently do not do.

evertheless she sounded a skeptical, cautionary note: "Modern man, like his primitive ancestors," she wrote, "still pays homage to the soothsayer who can offer a reassuring word and a bright future. And I am afraid that that is about all that most crystal gazers can supply, whether the bright future is there or not.... The lights are low, the price is high; the atmosphere is dim and the future is bright. But that future depends on what you do and not on the dazzling crystal."

On the other hand, the time-honored tradition of interpreting natural signs—observing the behavior of birds or the shape of clouds—can in fact yield scientifically valid information. Few today would deny that animals, plants, and the atmosphere itself form an interwoven ecological entity, of which one part may give clues to the whole. And the ancients, most of whom lived closer to the land than modern people, may have learned much about nature that we retain only as quaint nuggets of folklore.

In any case, we still exhibit a strong appetite for divination of many sorts. We may no longer inspect animal entrails for clues to what lies ahead, but many of us still attend crystal readings, stroll into Gypsy tearooms, or hang on every word of the long-range weather forecast. Like all mortals since the emergence of humankind, we fret about the future and yearn for signs of hope, for good things to come and for bad things to stay away.

Portents in the Palm

For thousands of years, in diverse cultures, people have believed that an individual's destiny is previewed in the hands, that every palm, from the time of birth, holds in its own unique network of mounts and valleys, lines and markings, the key to life's potential. It is also said that as the person matures, significant events in his or her life will be reflected in the palm. But these markers of the past and guideposts to the future are usually indecipherable to all but a few—those who can supposedly divine the course of someone's life through palm reading.

Palmistry has changed little over time. Its proponents claim that it enables people to understand themselves better. It may also reveal inherent strengths and weaknesses in character—useful knowledge when facing life's challenges—and provide clues as to how one's nature can affect health, career, and relationships. But most of all, many palmists contend, hand analysis enables people to make choices that will bring them pleasure and self-fulfillment.

In a reading, palmists usually compare the subject's right and left hands. The lines and overall form of the so-called passive hand are thought to reflect one's innate potential, while those of the dominant hand—typically the one used for writing—are said to reveal choices the individual has made and what may lie ahead. A thorough palmist generally discerns from the hand's shape and markings a likely life pattern, a set of tendencies, or particular events that may occur. Some of the features from which palmists gather information are examined on the next pages.

Observing the Hand

In palmistry, personality analysis is based on the appearance of the entire hand. Among the various factors taken into account in this overview, the basic form of the hand is particularly important.

Hands are often classified as one of four types, named by some practitioners of the art to correspond to the traditional four elements of nature—air, earth, water, and fire. The classifications are based on the shape of the palm and the length of the fingers in relation to it. Palms are typically rectangular or square, with either long or short fingers. Fingers are considered long if the middle finger (called the Saturn finger in palmistry) is at least as long as the palm itself, and short if that finger falls short of the palm's length.

Other factors that contribute to the hand's appearance are the shapes of the fingertips and the placement and flexibility of the thumb *(opposite page)*. To analyze the shape of your own hand, trace its outline on paper, then compare the drawing to those shown here.

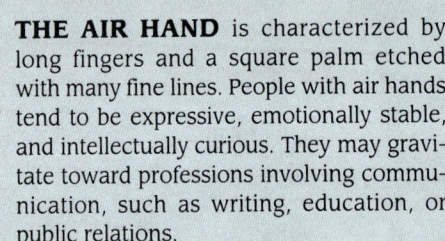

THE AIR HAND is characterized by long fingers and a square palm etched with many fine lines. People with air hands tend to be expressive, emotionally stable, and intellectually curious. They may gravitate toward professions involving communication, such as writing, education, or public relations.

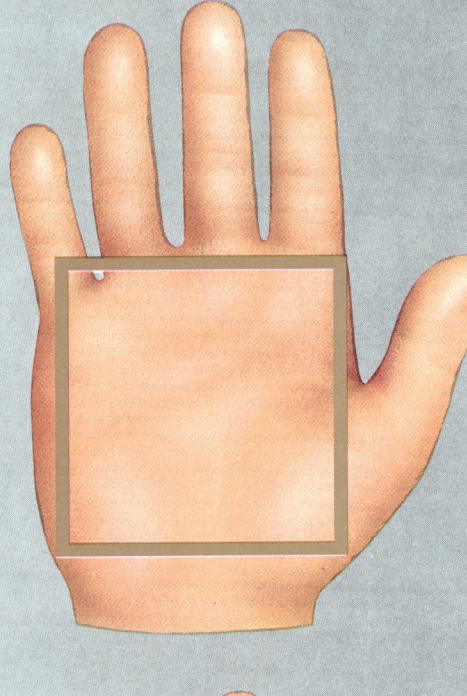

THE EARTH HAND, signified by a deeply lined square palm and short fingers, may reflect a serious, practical person who delights in physical activity. These individuals tend to enjoy manual occupations, such as carpentry, farming, and working with machinery.

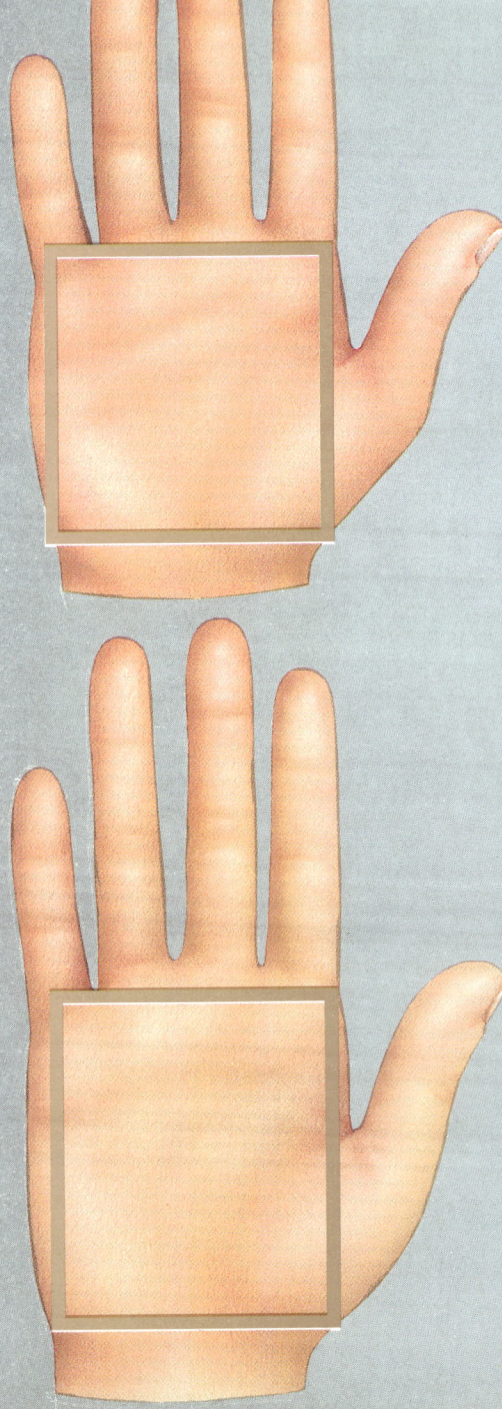

THE WATER HAND, with its long fingers extending from a finely lined rectangular palm, often reveals a sensitive, creative, quiet personality. Studious or relatively low-pressure occupations—such as research, office work, or retail sales—may appeal to these individuals.

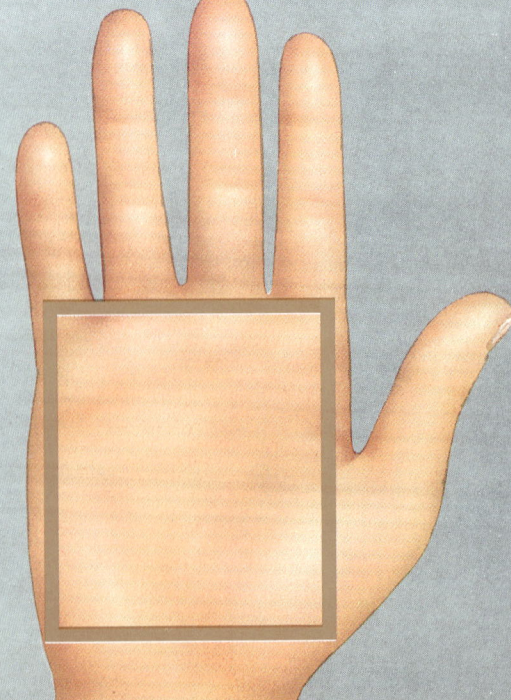

THE FIRE HAND, recognized by its short fingers and rectangular palm filled with clear lines, denotes an energetic, impetuous person. People who have fire hands seem drawn to professions that involve challenge, risk, and creativity, such as medicine, law enforcement, or the arts.

A Variety of Fingertips

The shape of an individual's fingertips, palmists maintain, provides further insight into his or her character. There are four distinct fingertip shapes—conic, round, square, and spatulate.

Conic fingertips, which taper off almost to a point, imply a sensitive and impulsive nature, as well as a love of art and beauty. The individual may also be highly intuitive, relying more on that gift than on powers of reason.

A well-balanced disposition is usually denoted by round fingertips. This individual adapts easily to change, is receptive to new ideas, and reacts to situations with equal measures of mental and emotional reasoning.

People with square fingertips tend to thrive on order and regularity and to express themselves clearly and with confidence. They desire security and stability for themselves as well as for their loved ones.

Fingertips that are narrow at the first joint and then flare to a wide tip are known as spatulate. Individuals with spatulate fingertips are usually considered to be independent, energetic, and enthusiastic; they love action everywhere in their lives, even seeking it in the books and other materials they read. These generally down-to-earth personalities often make true and loyal friends.

Palmists observe that some fingertip shapes are typically associated with certain hand types. Individuals with water hands, for example, frequently possess conic fingertips, while square fingertips are commonly found on individuals with air hands.

A mixture of one or more fingertip shapes on an individual's hand is also common. These so-called mixed hands suggest a person who is versatile, adapts quite easily to new situations, and may excel in a variety of occupations.

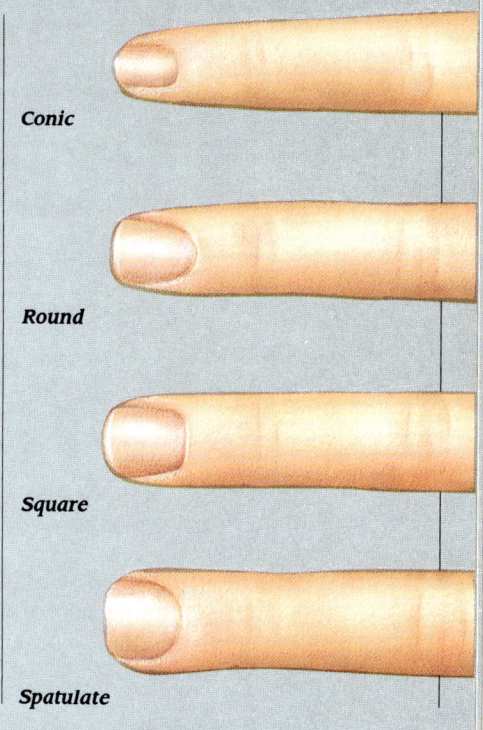

Conic

Round

Square

Spatulate

The Revealing Thumb

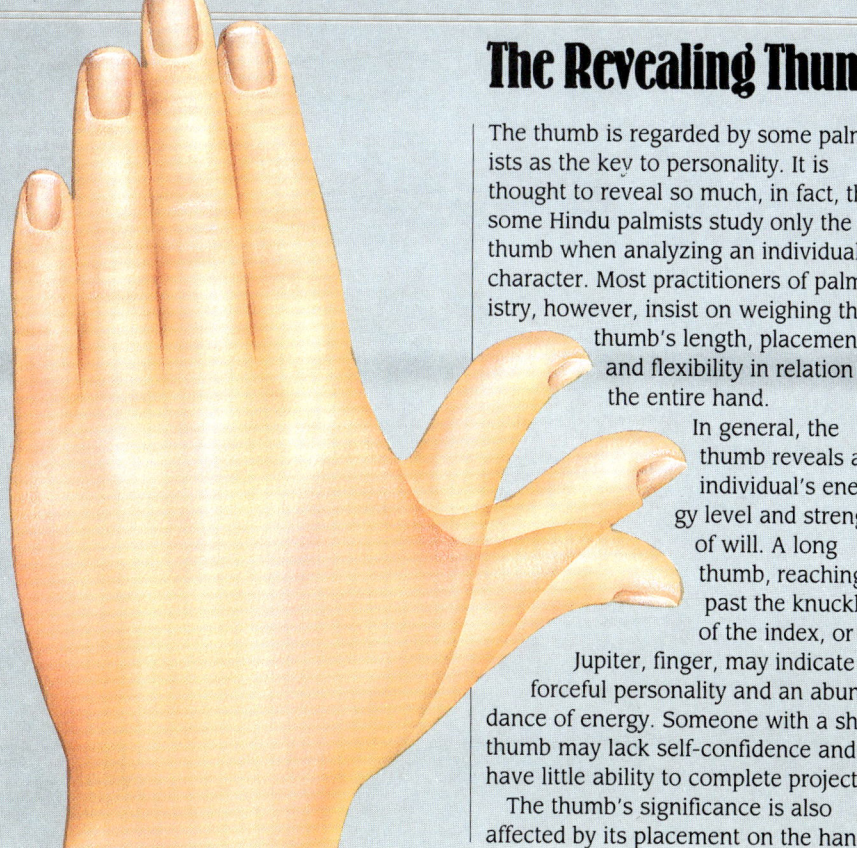

The thumb is regarded by some palmists as the key to personality. It is thought to reveal so much, in fact, that some Hindu palmists study only the thumb when analyzing an individual's character. Most practitioners of palmistry, however, insist on weighing the thumb's length, placement, and flexibility in relation to the entire hand.

In general, the thumb reveals an individual's energy level and strength of will. A long thumb, reaching past the knuckle of the index, or Jupiter, finger, may indicate a forceful personality and an abundance of energy. Someone with a short thumb may lack self-confidence and have little ability to complete projects.

The thumb's significance is also affected by its placement on the hand. A low-set thumb, one that creates an angle of sixty to ninety degrees between the thumb and index finger, reveals a personality that is flexible, independent, logical, and well-directed. Someone with a high-set thumb, creating an angle of thirty degrees or less with the index finger, may be tense and self-contained.

Another indication of ego strength is in the thumb's tip. If the tip is flexible, bending back easily at the first joint, the person probably adapts easily and is generous, although not indiscriminately so. If the thumb is extremely flexible, the individual might be extravagant or show a lack of restraint.

A thumb that bends only slightly under pressure may indicate a practical personality and a strong will modified by open-mindedness. The owner of a rigid thumb may be stubborn and resistant to new ideas and experiences. However, this person is usually very reliable, stable, and responsible.

Minding the Mounts

The most thorough readings by professional palmists may include an analysis of the palm's mounts, the fleshy pads found at the base of the thumb and each finger and on the outer edges of the palm. The larger the mount and the more directly it is centered under the corresponding finger, the greater its supposed influence on the personality. Prominent bulges are considered strong or highly developed mounts, while those that are flat or only slightly raised are judged normal or well developed. A depression in the palm instead of a fleshy pad constitutes a weak mount.

MOUNT OF SATURN. Found at the base of the middle, or Saturn, finger, this mount governs the introspective aspect of the personality. A well-developed Saturn mount reveals an independent nature, that of a person who enjoys solitude as well as the company of others. Self-awareness and emotional balance are indicated, as are fidelity and prudence.

A highly developed mount may indicate an unhealthy tendency toward self-absorption. And lack of a Saturn mount may denote indecisiveness, a pessimistic tendency, and a poor sense of humor.

MOUNT OF APOLLO. This mount, located at the base of the Apollo, or ring, finger, is said to govern all forms of creativity. A well-developed mount implies strong artistic abilities and a love of beauty. These talents may not apply solely to the fine arts but may also include culinary expertise or other forms of expression. A prominent Apollo mount may signify a tendency toward extravagance and materialism as well as vanity and self-indulgence. Low physical energy, a lack of aesthetic values, and a disregard for creative pursuits may stem from a weak Apollo mount.

MOUNT OF JUPITER. At the base of the index finger, the mount of Jupiter reveals an individual's degree of self-confidence, social sense, and leadership ability. If the mount is well developed, healthy measures of assertiveness and ambition are indicated, as well as an even temper, generosity, and self-assurance.

An unusually strong mount may tip the scales toward vanity, narcissism, and an overbearing attitude. However, if the prominent mount is modified by factors in the lines and fingers, the individual may simply exhibit strong leadership skills. An underdeveloped mount may suggest a poor self-image, lack of respect for authority, and a tendency toward idleness.

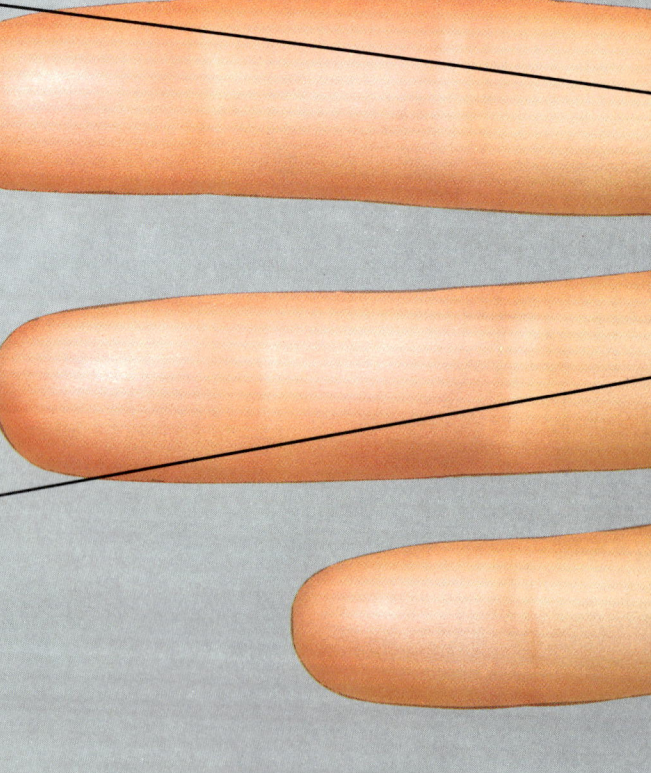

MOUNT OF MERCURY. Communication is ruled by the mount of Mercury, at the base of the pinkie. A well-developed mount implies a talent for self-expression and a lively disposition. A large mount has no negative connotations, but an underdeveloped one may mean a lack of business acumen and difficulty communicating. A mount with short, straight lines may denote a caring, compassionate nature.

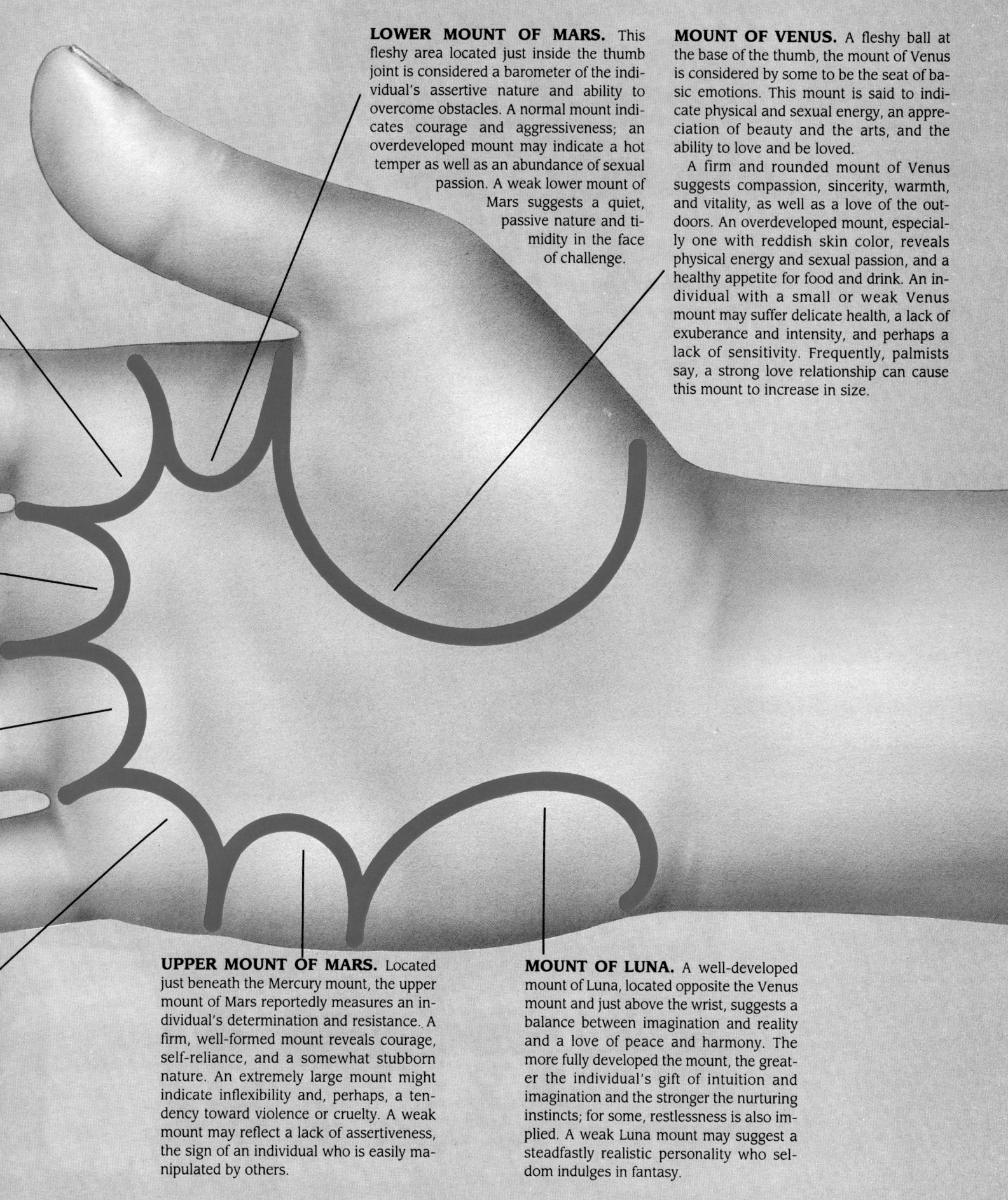

LOWER MOUNT OF MARS. This fleshy area located just inside the thumb joint is considered a barometer of the individual's assertive nature and ability to overcome obstacles. A normal mount indicates courage and aggressiveness; an overdeveloped mount may indicate a hot temper as well as an abundance of sexual passion. A weak lower mount of Mars suggests a quiet, passive nature and timidity in the face of challenge.

MOUNT OF VENUS. A fleshy ball at the base of the thumb, the mount of Venus is considered by some to be the seat of basic emotions. This mount is said to indicate physical and sexual energy, an appreciation of beauty and the arts, and the ability to love and be loved.

A firm and rounded mount of Venus suggests compassion, sincerity, warmth, and vitality, as well as a love of the outdoors. An overdeveloped mount, especially one with reddish skin color, reveals physical energy and sexual passion, and a healthy appetite for food and drink. An individual with a small or weak Venus mount may suffer delicate health, a lack of exuberance and intensity, and perhaps a lack of sensitivity. Frequently, palmists say, a strong love relationship can cause this mount to increase in size.

UPPER MOUNT OF MARS. Located just beneath the Mercury mount, the upper mount of Mars reportedly measures an individual's determination and resistance. A firm, well-formed mount reveals courage, self-reliance, and a somewhat stubborn nature. An extremely large mount might indicate inflexibility and, perhaps, a tendency toward violence or cruelty. A weak mount may reflect a lack of assertiveness, the sign of an individual who is easily manipulated by others.

MOUNT OF LUNA. A well-developed mount of Luna, located opposite the Venus mount and just above the wrist, suggests a balance between imagination and reality and a love of peace and harmony. The more fully developed the mount, the greater the individual's gift of intuition and imagination and the stronger the nurturing instincts; for some, restlessness is also implied. A weak Luna mount may suggest a steadfastly realistic personality who seldom indulges in fantasy.

Looking at the Lines

The complex network of lines discernible in every palm is allegedly capable of steering each of us along life's course. Palmists analyze these lines not only to reflect the development of an individual's character traits as he or she matures but also to reveal insights into the future. And armed with this knowledge, the believers say, a person can actually affect future events. The lines of the palm are constantly changing: Old lines may fade or grow clearer and new ones may appear, sometimes in a matter of weeks. By modifying behavior and changing attitudes, palmists maintain, we can change our lines—and thus our lives—to achieve our predestined potential.

HEART LINE. An ideal heart line, indicating a warm and demonstrative nature, begins at the hand's outer edge, beneath the Mercury finger. It traverses the palm near the base of the finger mounts, curving upward slightly before ending between the Jupiter and Saturn mounts.

An upward curve implies a physical or instinctual sexuality, while a straight heart line suggests that romantic imagery is important in love. Two or three branches at the line's end are thought to indicate a balance between emotions, realism, and physical passion.

A wide space between the heart and head lines reflects extroversion and an unconventional outlook on life; a narrow space might imply some lack of self-confidence, difficulty expressing feelings, and a secretive nature. If the heart line is longer than the head line, the person could be ruled more by emotions than reason.

A chainlike heart line may signal a person who falls in love easily but fears commitment. Romantic upsets are suggested by short diagonal lines crossing the heart line; small islands—points where the line splits in two, then merges once more—especially near the Jupiter mount, could imply significant romantic disappointments, such as divorce.

RELATIONSHIP LINES. On the outer edge of the hand, between the heart line and the base of the Mercury finger, one or more short, horizontal lines may be found. Called relationship or marriage lines, they supposedly indicate important commitments. The lines can signify deep friendships as well as intimate relationships. The stronger the line, it is said, the more potential for the union.

HEAD LINE. The head line, reflecting intellectual capacity and potential, usually begins below the Jupiter mount and traverses the palm. An analytical nature is typified by a straight head line, while a downward-sloping line suggests creativity. A forked end indicates a balance between imagination and realism.

Average intelligence and good reasoning powers are symbolized by a head line stretching at least two-thirds of the way across the palm. A longer line is said to reveal keen insight and a range of intellectual interests. A wide gap between the head and life lines at their origin may reflect impulsivity and impatience; the closer the lines, the more tentative the person.

Lines denoting current or past relationships are usually indelibly etched in the palm, but those signaling future ones may change periodically. A line may become clearer to show deeper feelings, or new lines may appear. To estimate the age at which a relationship may occur, note the line's position between the heart line and the base of the Mercury finger; a point about midway may mean age thirty-five.

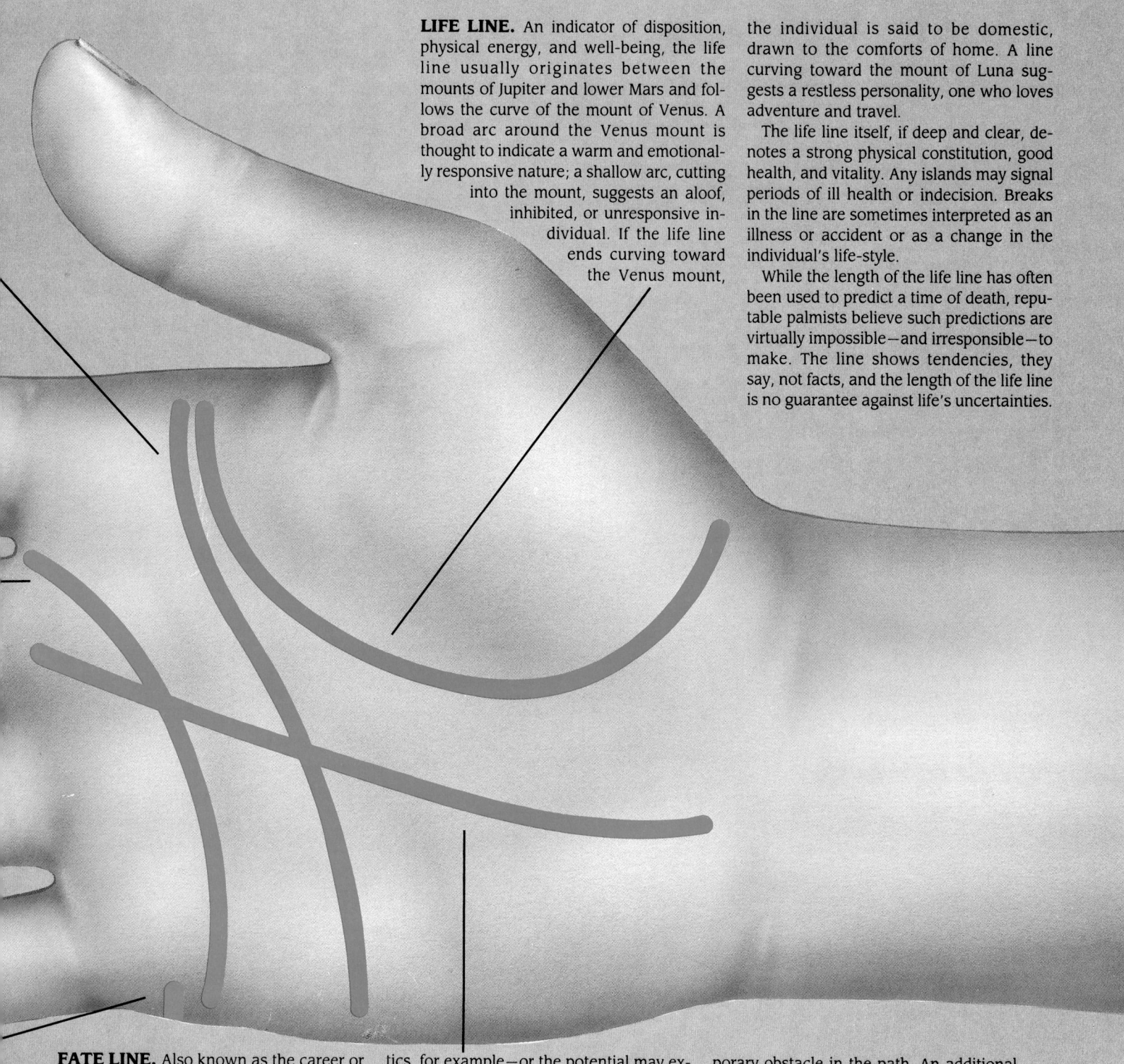

LIFE LINE. An indicator of disposition, physical energy, and well-being, the life line usually originates between the mounts of Jupiter and lower Mars and follows the curve of the mount of Venus. A broad arc around the Venus mount is thought to indicate a warm and emotionally responsive nature; a shallow arc, cutting into the mount, suggests an aloof, inhibited, or unresponsive individual. If the life line ends curving toward the Venus mount, the individual is said to be domestic, drawn to the comforts of home. A line curving toward the mount of Luna suggests a restless personality, one who loves adventure and travel.

The life line itself, if deep and clear, denotes a strong physical constitution, good health, and vitality. Any islands may signal periods of ill health or indecision. Breaks in the line are sometimes interpreted as an illness or accident or as a change in the individual's life-style.

While the length of the life line has often been used to predict a time of death, reputable palmists believe such predictions are virtually impossible—and irresponsible—to make. The line shows tendencies, they say, not facts, and the length of the life line is no guarantee against life's uncertainties.

FATE LINE. Also known as the career or destiny line, this line reveals an individual's level of satisfaction with a profession or other chosen task. Ideally, the fate line begins just above the wrist and moves upward toward the mount of Saturn. Generally, the higher in the palm the fate line begins, the later in life the person will find his or her true vocation.

If the fate line originates in the mount of Luna, it portends a career that depends on the decisions of other people—as in politics, for example—or the potential may exist for a number of careers and possible relocation. If the line arises from the mount of Venus, the family may play a part in the individual's profession.

The more content an individual is with his or her chosen path, the clearer the fate line may be; a weak, fragmented line may reveal a person who feels restless or unfulfilled. Breaks in the fate line are interpreted as a hiatus in one's career or a change of direction, and islands may reveal a temporary obstacle in the path. An additional vertical line running close to the fate line may suggest a second career or strong avocational interest.

A person will remain active throughout life, it is thought, if he or she possesses a long fate line. If the line comes to a stop at the heart line, however, the individual's ambition could be thwarted by emotions; if the line ends at the head line, his or her success may be stymied by some sort of intellectual blunder.

A Sampling of Readings

Palmistry is an art acquired through study and patience, and skillful observation is essential to a responsible reading. During a hand analysis, a reputable palmist will carefully examine the various features of the fingers and hands discussed on the previous pages. He or she will also observe the dozens of other markings of the palm, since even the most subtle striation may be imbued with special meaning. Each element is usually described separately, then discussed in the context of the entire hand.

Although most palmists agree on the significance of the palm's major markings, interpretations may vary somewhat from one reader to another. The palm prints of a man and two women, along with brief readings based on the most prominent features—all prepared by professional palmist Nathaniel Altman—appear on the following pages.

SENSITIVITY IN A HAND. The palm print of this twenty-six-year-old woman reveals a sensuous nature. The heart line is very long, indicating a person who is sensitive and humane. She tends to fall in love easily and may be guided more by her heart than her head in relationships with others. Lines at the base of the Mercury finger indicate three important relationships, one probably at an earlier age and two that may lie in the future. These could also be close friendships.

A high level of physical and emotional energy is indicated by the firm, large mount of Venus. The life line is also fairly strong but has some overlappings; this could signal a need to pay more attention to health. The life line touches the head line at its origin, implying a high-strung nature. This is compounded by the large number of fine lines in the palm, suggesting a sensitivity to stress.

A balance between imagination and realism is indicated by the split at the end of the head line, and the downward slope of one branch toward the mount of Luna suggests good instinctual ability. The Luna mount is well developed, reinforcing both the imaginative and the intuitive traits.

Several career lines are visible in the palm. This could indicate literally more than one career, or a very important hobby or volunteer work in addition to a profession. The long fingers, typical of an air hand, show an ability to focus on details; the Jupiter finger is slightly longer than the Apollo, suggesting a take-charge personality. Although the Mercury finger is long, a mark of good communication, it is slightly twisted, signaling a need to be more direct with others. The thumb is rather rigid, showing a tendency to be stubborn but also responsible and reliable.

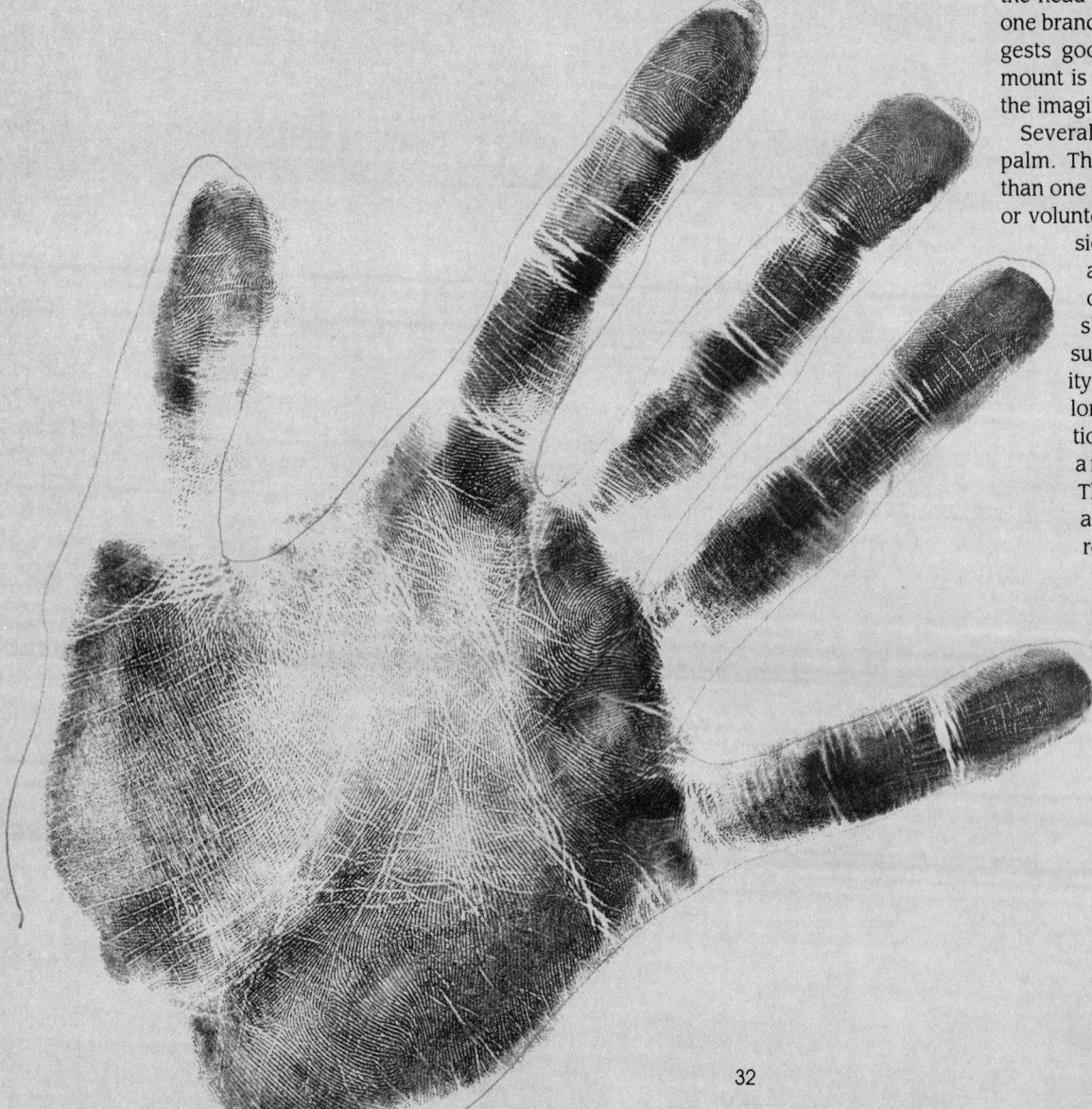

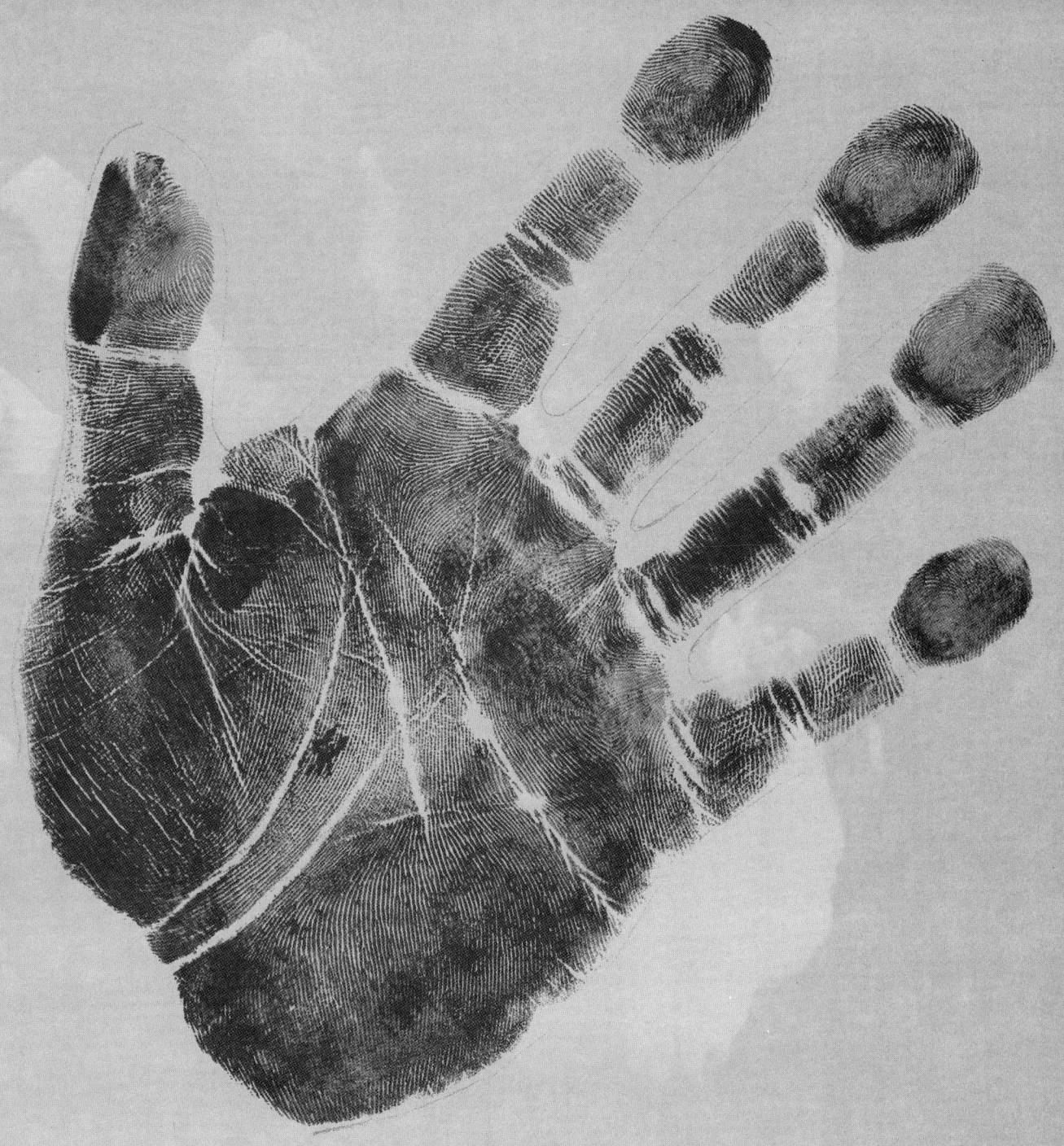

A SIMPLE DOWN-TO-EARTH HAND. The square palm and short fingers of this earth hand suggest that this twenty-eight-year-old loves the outdoors and is physically oriented. The round fingertips signal a fairly even disposition, but the thumb is rather stiff, so he may tend to be stubborn. A long and straight Mercury finger indicates that he is a good communicator, while a Jupiter finger that is shorter than the Apollo finger may mean a lack of self-esteem.

The mount of Venus, at the base of the thumb, is large and well developed, signifying an abundance of physical energy and passion. A good measure of instinct and a protective nature are revealed in the large mount of Luna, and a strong upper mount of Mars suggests a lot of resistance but also a good deal of courage. The lower Mars mount is prominent, too, reflecting assertiveness and, possibly, a short temper.

The major lines of the hand are deep and well defined, and there is a lack of small, spidery lines. This suggests a simplified way of viewing things—a clear and direct approach, narrow in scope, rather than an all-encompassing philosophical view—and a lesser degree of sensitivity. But these characteristics are modified, in part, by a long heart line, which reveals a generous, loving nature. The small branches at the beginning of the line, under the Mercury finger, reflect some sensitivity in the personality, particularly in the younger years.

The head line, strong, clear, and of average length, shows a good ability to assess situations and a strong sense of purpose. The life line has no major breaks or islands, suggesting good health and vitality.

A particularly clear fate line indicates involvement in one career for a long time. The split in the line above the head line is a sign of dual careers—and indeed, in this case, the young man is an automobile mechanic who also sells automotive parts.

Just below the mount of Mercury is a fairly long relationship line, reflecting his happy marriage. Just below that line, barely visible in this hand print, is a line from an earlier union, which ended in divorce.

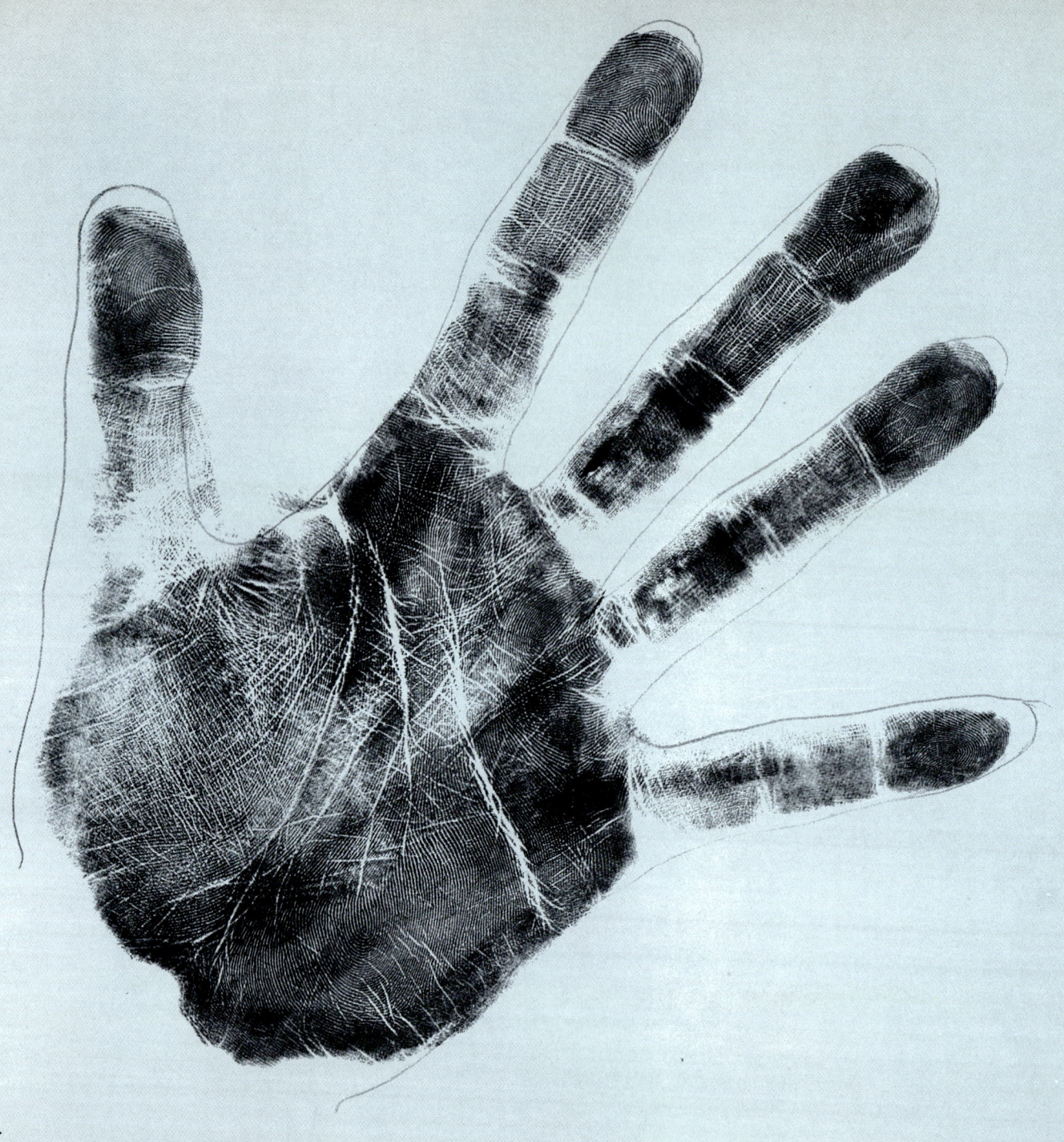

AN ARTIST'S HAND. The long, thin fingers and rectangular palm of this woman, a thirty-five-year-old artist, reveal the patience, attention to detail, and intellectual nature typical of a water hand. The Mercury finger tapers to a point at the tip, reflecting sensitivity and a love of art and beauty. It is also very long and straight, indicating good communication, a trait that is underscored by a well-developed Mercury mount.

The head line is strong and forked at its end, denoting a balance between realism and imagination, and its downward slope toward the mount of Luna reveals a creative intellect. Good imagination and instinct are suggested by a prominent Luna mount, and those traits are strengthened by a skin ridge pattern that appears to connect the two branches at the end of the head line. Instinctual abilities are also seen in the small diagonal lines moving up from the Luna mount toward the center of the palm. A good measure of self-reliance is indicated by the space between the head and life lines, but there is also a tendency to be impulsive.

The life line itself is fairly long, but some islands appear about the time of middle age; this suggests a need to be mindful of health then. The line forms a wide arc around the mount of Venus, reflecting a warm and sensual nature. Near the life line's end, a branch moving toward the mount of Luna implies restlessness. This coincides with the short horizontal lines at the palm's outer edge, indicating the potential for travel.

The heart line, which ends between the Jupiter and Saturn fingers, suggests a generous, sympathetic spirit, but also a good balance between reason and emotions. The heart line is somewhat chained, revealing sensitivity, emotional intensity, and a vulnerability to hurt.

Penmanship and Personality

Most handwriting analysts wince when their work is compared with divination. They practice a science and an art, they say; they are psychologists, not psychics. And indeed, forensic graphology—used, among other things, to detect forgery and establish authenticity of manuscripts—is widely recognized as legitimate science. More questionable, however, is the contention of many graphologists that they can deduce character traits from a sample of script. And it is in this nebulous area that they share with many diviners at least one aim: Both bend their labors toward extracting the essence of personality.

Graphologists emphasize that character reveals itself in handwriting by way of innumerable small clues, each one of which must be considered in conjunction with all the others. With proper attention to detail, they say, graphology can assess more than 300 personality characteristics, among them sociability or introversion, egocentricity, imagination, ambition, and enthusiasm.

Nevertheless, experts warn that graphology can yield only clues, not certainties, about character. But the same could be said of more traditional psychological yardsticks. Psychologist David Lester, who did an extensive study pitting graphology against standard tests such as the Minnesota Multiphasic Personality Inventory and the Rorschach inkblot, found that graphology was just as accurate as its more orthodox competition in assessing personality.

Some of the basic principles of graphology, along with an analysis of two writing samples, appear on the following pages.

Different Slants

Lincoln's Gettysburg Address

Four score and seven years ago our fathers brought forth on this continent, a new nation, conceived in liberty, and dedicated to the proposition that all men are created equal.

Most people learned as schoolchildren to write according to the Palmer Method, shown above in an exerpt from the Gettysburg Address. This standard, devised by educator Austin N. Palmer in the nineteenth century, is still used by handwriting experts as a control against which other scripts are measured.

No one mimics for long the tedious perfection prescribed by Palmer. Each individual adapts, embellishes, and eliminates until a handwriting style emerges that is as distinctive and specific as a fingerprint. Graphologists attribute this diversity to the uniqueness of each human brain. The brain, they say, does the writing; the hands are only the tools. Therefore, each person's writing can be seen as a kind of psychological logbook.

To read it, experts prefer to work from writing that is spontaneous—not copied—and inscribed on unlined paper. They look first at general characteristics, including the slant of the letters, their height and depth, the slope of the line, and the way words are spaced.

Script that slants to the right supposedly denotes a person pulled toward others, an individual who wants and needs human contact. The greater the slant, the greater the need for approval. A negative aspect of the forward slant is that its owner may be overly emotional, especially under stress. A backward slant reveals a loner, an introspective person who may overcontrol emotions. An erratic slant—letters leaning first one way, then another—connotes versatility, but also moodiness and instability.

Graphologists divide lines of script horizontally into three zones, illustrated by the heavy lines in the sample above. The proportional distribution of the letters within the zones can be telling. The upper zone governs intellect, spirituality, idealism, and imagination. The middle zone pertains to practical functions related to work and family and social interactions. The lower zone shows attitudes about physicality, sex, and material matters. Letters apportioned evenly through all three zones reveal inner harmony. If upper loops on such letters as *f, h, k,* and *l* show outsized height, the writer is apt to be idealistic and prone to daydream. Writing dominated by the middle zone purportedly implies a self-involved person who lives for the moment. Deep stretches into the lower zone denote strong physical and material drives.

The slope of a line of script is also said to be significant. Writing that marches directly from left margin to right reveals someone self-contained, even-tempered, and goal-directed. Writing rising toward the end of a line purportedly suggests optimism or exhilaration. And a sample that slopes downward shows pessimism, depression, or fatigue.

Spacing between words can reveal certain social and emotional tendencies. Narrow spacing implies a need for social contact, possibly leading to a certain lack of discrimination in choosing friends. Wide spacing reflects reserve and caution; the writer is metaphorically distancing himself or herself from others. Moderate spacing indicates a happy medium, a person who is both self-sufficient and sociable.

Another big-picture item the graphologist might address is the size of the writing. Large script denotes an expansive ego; medium-size writing a balanced, reasonable, and adaptable person; small writing a rationalist, possibly a scientist or academic. Very small writing that tends to flatten into a line denotes feelings of inferiority, while script that varies in size indicates moodiness and extreme sensitivity.

Different Strokes

After assessing the overall character of a handwriting style, the graphologist proceeds to the wealth of minutiae yielded by individual letters and strokes.

Capital letters are said to be clues to one's ego, the face one presents to the world. Large, overblown capitals, for instance, reveal a need for attention and admiration, while small ones suggest excessive modesty and a lack of self-assurance. Scroll-like, much-embellished capitals denote vulgarity; simple printed capitals good taste. The capital personal pronoun *I* is a particularly important benchmark of one's self-assessment. An *I* much larger than other capitals indicates self-interest and a confident facade that may mask uncertainty. A small, badly shaped *I* bespeaks self-consciousness and weak will. A very round *I* is self-protective and introverted, but an *I* that is large and angular shows an abrasive egotism.

I is also significant in the lower case, where its dot supposedly presents innumerable clues to character. For example, if the *i* has an elongated dot, the writer is probably highly sensitive with an acute critical sense. A thick, heavy dot indicates bad temper, possibly to the point of brutality. A light dot riding high above the *i*'s stem shows refinement and imagination.

A few more of the multitudinous clues that a good graphologist pursues are depicted on this page.

For all of graphology's breadth and attention to detail, however, there are two basic characteristics that the practice chronically fails to detect with any certainty: age and sex. It seems that maturity does not always parallel chronology, and most people have characteristics of both genders within their psychological makeup.

STARTS AND FINISHES

Long approach strokes to first letters can show attachment to the past. The small initial hook and long sweep into the f—significantly, in the word father—show someone seeking to retrieve the past.

Contrasting with the previous f, this one is without preamble. When there is no approach stroke at all, the writer is probably a direct, forward-looking, and efficient person.

The little upward flourish on the r indicates generosity, along with a possible interest in such matters as religion, theoretical reasoning, or abstract thinking.

The slight inward hook on the final y is tiny, but telling. It betokens a certain tenacity and persistence. The writer is probably also goal oriented and somewhat acquisitive.

THE LETTER T

On writing that slants to the left, a single long t-bar that crosses two stems shows willpower, mental agility, and possible executive ability.

The t-bar that loops backward to cross the stem reveals guilt feelings, though they might well be groundless.

Crossing a t above the stem bespeaks goals that may be too lofty. The bar's position left of the stem signals hesitancy or procrastination.

A t crossed low on the stem denotes a pedestrian thinker, one who sets safe, easy goals and takes refuge in the tried and tested.

A t-bar that slants upward, like a whole line of script edging upward, suggests an optimistic outlook on life.

The abrupt downward slant of this t-bar indicates a writer who is stubborn and willful and inclined to be overly critical.

Revelations in Script

The handwriting samples shown here were analyzed by Gloria Weiss, a forensic graphologist and graphology teacher based in Washington, D.C. The sample below was provided by a young mother and professional woman, the one on the facing page by a man who became a novelist after retiring from government.

Lincoln's Gettysburg Address

Four score and seven years ago our fathers brought forth upon this continent a new ~~so~~ nation, conceived in liberty, and dedicated to this proposition that all men are created equal.

The slant and fluidity of this sample give the overall impression of spontaneity, enthusiasm, versatility, imagination, directness, and efficiency. A variability in the size and shape of the writing suggests occasional moodiness and indicates the writer is often pressed for time.

The slightly arched t-bars denote concerted mental effort to control concentration that tends to be scattered; but on the positive side, a small flourish to the bars bespeaks a good sense of humor. The word spacing varies from close to comparatively wide. This means the writer knows how to be close to people without being intrusive. Innate good taste and quiet self-confidence show in the capital letters, which are sizable, but also simple, direct, and unassuming. The upward slope of the writing reveals an optimistic nature. Varied interests show in the way the writing balances fairly evenly across the three zones. But the middle zone is a little small, and projections into the upper and lower zones vary. These factors suggest the writer may have trouble with priorities and focus as she tries to juggle the diverse concerns in her life.

In the words *conceived, liberty,* and *proposition,* Weiss notes the script's tendency to begin large and taper down toward the end of a word. This is a habit that implies diplomacy and tact. In writing that is more thready and less defined, these virtues might change to hypocrisy, Weiss says.

However, the tapering here must be balanced against the ovals of the small *a*'s and *o*'s. The ovals are clearly formed and usually fully closed at the top, showing honesty and directness. Weiss concludes the writer is neither insincere nor manipulative, but she tends to temporize with the truth a bit to avoid hurting other people's feelings.

In which is Gettysburg Address

Four score and seven years ago our fathers brought forth upon this continent a new nation, conceived in liberty, and dedicated to the proposition that all men are created equal.

This writing shows a slight leftward slant, a singular regularity, and very straight alignment, marching left to right with precision and purpose. The writer is exceptionally goal directed, Weiss says. He is single-minded and tenacious in his aims; once he plots a course he will not deviate from it. He finishes what he starts, and he finishes on time.

This general observation is confirmed by smaller details, such as the writer's formation of the small letter *f*. The lowercase *f* is especially important to graphologists in what it reveals about organizational ability. According to Weiss, a well-balanced *f* whose upper and lower extensions are fairly equal—as those in the novelist's *f*'s are—almost guarantees that the writer has a strong sense of organization. Moreover, he is judicious. Wide spacing between his lines betokens a man who weighs and considers carefully before deciding or acting.

The upper zone dominates his script; the lowercase *l*'s and *b*'s have upward extensions that soar well out of proportion to the small middle zone. Here is a man of theory and intellect, more at home in the realm of ideas than with practical, mundane matters.

Nevertheless, certain clues imply the writer is not quite as rigid as an overall reading suggests. The odd reversal in the lower arm of his *f* shows flexibility, and the rightward t-bars indicate considerable enthusiasm and some spontaneity. Despite a certain standoffishness in the script's leftward slant, long final strokes on some of the letters show a degree of extroversion, a reaching out toward others. The simplicity of the capitals says the writer is no egotist. His good taste precludes presumption.

Still, he wants and expects a lot from life. Where the young mother writes with rather light pressure, the man bears down on his words. This shows strong drive and a will to achieve.

F f 1 2 3 4 5 6 7 8 9 0

Charting the Four Basic Numbers

In the ancient practice of numerology, a person's birth chart consists of four basic numbers—three drawn from the name given at birth and one from the birth date. Numerologists analyze these numbers to discover clues about the individual's character, destiny, and life cycles. A personal chart reading, similar to those performed by professionals, can be done by simply calculating these four numbers and checking the capsule descriptions on the following pages. Although people are the usual subjects, the process can be applied to anything that has a name and date of birth or origin—a cat, a business, a nation, or even an idea.

The first step in this intriguing exercise is to translate the name into its numerical equivalent, using the number-letter conversion table shown on the opposite page. Each letter is assigned a single-digit number based on its sequential place in the alphabet: The letters *A* through *I* are numbered one through nine, with the remaining letters reduced to one of those digits through simple addition. For example, *J* as the tenth letter reduces to a one (10=1+0=1), and *U* as the twenty-first letter reduces to a three (21=2+1=3).

The three birth-name numbers are determined by adding the numerical values of three different sets of letters in the name: first, all the vowels that occur; then, all the consonants; and finally, the total of all the letters. The numerical total of the vowels—*a, e, i, o,* and *u*—in the name is called the Soul Number. This is thought to reflect the person's true inner self, encompassing ambitions and motivations, judgment and attitudes, and feelings. The total of the consonants, on the other hand, produces the Outer Personality Number, which relates to physical appearance, health, and the impression the person makes on others through dress and behavior.

The total of the entire birth name is known as the Path of Destiny Number. It indicates the sum of the individual's capabilities and achievements and how he or she will affect others. The Path of Destiny Number also influences the course a person will take to attain career goals—whether the career involves raising a family or running a corporation—and describes the types of people who will be encountered along the way.

Numerologists believe that although the birth name remains the foundation of nature and destiny throughout life, a name change can dramatically alter the mix of letters and numbers and thus expand the person's experiences, attitudes, and role in society. A woman who changes her last name at marriage, for example, may become more adaptable and flexible in her new circumstances because she is taking on a new set of numbers that will be used along with her birth name. Numerology points to a shift in personal numbers as a factor in such transformations. Similarly, movie stars and writers may take on new public identities—and private personalities—through name changes they hope will provide a certain image. Archibald Leach and Joyce Frankenburg certainly have a different ring from Cary Grant and Jane Seymour, the stage names these two performers chose.

Although a person's name may change over the course of a lifetime, the birth date is constant. And it is the sum of numbers in this date that produces the fourth and most important number in a numerology chart—the Life Lesson Number. This number reveals the lessons and truths a person is meant to learn during his lifetime; it signals the essential purpose of his existence.

The Life Lesson Number is obtained by writing the birth date in numbers and totaling them until they reduce to a single digit. If your birth date is November 4, 1947, for example, you would figure your Life Lesson Number by writing the date as 11-4-1947—making sure to use the full year, not the abbreviation '47—and then adding the digits until they reduce to a nine (1+1+4+1+9+4+7=27=2+7=9).

The birth-date number is also the key to interpreting what numerologists call "personal-year cycles"—a set of reigning patterns and influences such as assertiveness, harmony, security, resignation, and the like. These patterns are said to be set in motion on the day a person is born and continue in nine-year cycles for as long as he or she lives. The personal-year cycle explains where energy should be focused during any given twelve-month period—a kind of psychic homework assignment for the year.

A simple method of determining the current personal-year cycle is to go back to the person's last birthday and add the numbers in that date, as demonstrated above. The patterns associated with this number will prevail from that birthday up to the next birthday, and then the cycle will move forward one number; at the end of year nine in the cycle, the person begins again with year one.

Whatever Life Lesson Number is determined on the day of birth, that number is repeated in the person's ninth year—and every nine years thereafter. For this reason, the birth year and the ages of 9, 18, 27, 36, 45, 54, and so on are important years—periods when events occur that underscore the major theme of a person's life and remind him again of the lessons he is here to learn.

Once the four numbers in a personal birth chart are determined, the final step is to look up their interpretations. Each of the numerical descriptions on the following pages begins with the number's supposed essence, followed by its influence as a personal number in one of the four categories. If you are examining your Soul Number, for example, the definition describes your inner nature. If it is your Outer Personality Number, the description represents how others see you. If you are looking up your Path of Destiny Number, the influence applies to your career course. And if it is your Life Lesson Number, the definition suggests the lessons you need to learn. And finally, the personal-year cycle describes the prevailing pattern of events and attitudes for any year—past, present, or future.

Essence of One: Activation. One is the seed, the beginning, when the life force is self-compelled to move out to explore and confront newness. It is original and individualistic because it is uninfluenced by previous experience. Because it does not know that things cannot be done, it proceeds with complete faith to do them. One is the pioneer, facing the unknown with an innocent courage. It draws upon its own creative well to solve any problems that arise.

Personal Number One: You are an extreme individualist and a self-motivator, and therefore feel comfortable following your own ideas and instincts. Your individuality is the drive behind your need for freedom and independence. You express leadership creatively and with originality. Not wanting to take a secondary position, you handle the entire operation and leave the details to others. You learn more from experience than from instruction and advice, which you dislike. Your ardent nature can cause swings in your emotional behavior. Yet the intensity of your focus, together with your courage and intelligence, make you a tower of inspiration in difficult times. You should avoid becoming arrogant, selfish, and stubborn.

Personal-Year-Cycle One: This is the beginning of a new nine-year cycle in your life. Major changes have occurred and you are still in the process of sorting them out physically and emotionally. You feel compelled to center on yourself, which may be a difficult mental transition if you have been trained to think of others first. However, your needs should come first now—the decisions you make during this cycle will influence your life for the next four to nine years. Even if there are people around you, you may feel isolated and alone. Do not let this be a concern, because your sense of separation allows you to make important decisions uninfluenced by others. People may offer advice, but you will not take it. You feel more independent, assertive, and willing to take chances. This is the year to express your individuality, to attempt those things you have only dreamed of to this point. One important person, attracted by your new attitude, may come into your life.

Essence of Two: Attraction. In its dynamic advancement, One is attracted to another One, and they become Two. Two is the gestation period where the seed from One is collected and assimilated, and things begin to form. It is the mirror of illumination where knowledge comes from opposites: night and day, female and male. Two is the principle of marriage between two distinct entities.

Personal Number Two: You are a diplomat with a strong desire for peace and harmony. Since you are so strongly tuned in to the moods and feelings of others, you collect and assimilate their ideas, which can make it difficult for you to make decisions. You are so sensitive that you naturally interact with others gently while staying in the background and remaining unobtrusive. The subtle forces of nature stir you deeply; music and other soothing art forms fulfill your deep sense of rhythm and harmony. You have an expansive imagination that creates a magic mirror in which you can see every detail. Your cooperative and patient nature, along with your sincerity and your ability to see both sides of things, makes you the perfect partner. Avoid oversensitivity, indecision, and feelings of inferiority.

Personal-Year-Cycle Two: This year requires a calm, receptive attitude on your part. Because you have the ability to see opposing points of view now, you become the peacemaker or mediator. You become aware of the needs of others and are willing to settle any differences that may have arisen as a result of last year's assertiveness. You may find it hard to make decisions now, preferring to remain more in the background. This is a good period for partnerships because of your sensitivity. Marriage may occur during this cycle. Your subconscious is very active, so you should explore and develop your intuitive abilities. Flashes of insight and understanding will aid you in solving difficult situations. Sudden recognition is possible for some act or work you are presently doing or perhaps have long forgotten. Legal dealings, sales agreements, legacies, and claims may occur now. It is a curious year, when life flows along quietly—until sudden, exciting events occur that can require overnight decisions. Your motto this year should be: Expect the unexpected. And listen to your inner self. Creative magic lies waiting to be explored.

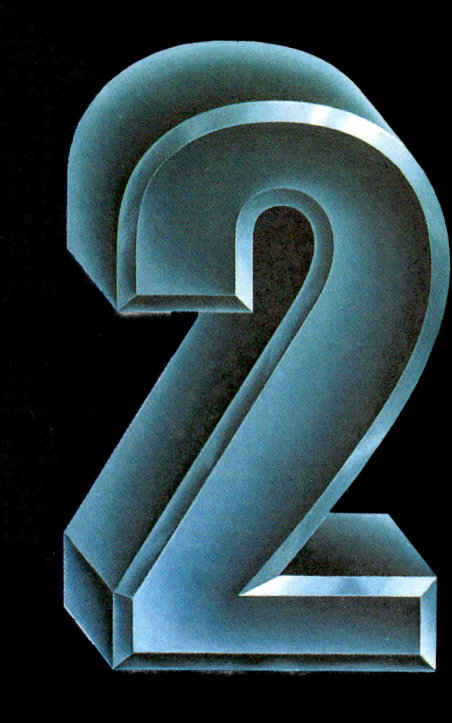

Essence of Three: Expansion. The marriage of Two results in growth and unfoldment in Three. The most imaginative and creative of the numbers, Three is the mother-father-child. This family unit is symbolized by the triangle, known as the first perfect shape in mathematics—that is, the first closed plane that can be constructed with straight lines. The triangle represents the three-fold nature of divinity in most cultures.

Personal Number Three: You are an extremely expressive individual who can influence others with your ability to communicate in a flamboyant style. Somewhere there is a stage waiting for you. Whether you are speaking, writing, or acting, your bright, warm nature draws others who bask in your enthusiasm and energy. You are aware of your appearance because performing depends upon the impression you make on others. You dream big, and your faith is often rewarded because positive thinking produces positive results. Because of your expansive nature, you meet people from different cultures and social strata, increasing your already broad and all-encompassing thinking. Do not scatter your energies, and avoid exaggeration, self-indulgence, and foolish optimism.

Personal-Year-Cycle Three: This is your year of activity, expansion, travel, and luck. You need room to move and express yourself, to experience life, freedom, and the joy of living. You may travel to another part of this land or to another country and meet people who enlarge your idea of the world. Some of the individuals you meet now can be important business contacts in the future. You are aware of your appearance and may indulge in a new wardrobe, hairstyle, or other beauty improvements. Since this is often called a lucky cycle, your one ticket may win the prize. But do not overindulge. Overexpansion leads to bankruptcy. If you use good judgment, however, this is a fertile cycle that could include the birth of a child, a creation of the mind, or an expansion of your bank account. In the midst of this social cycle, you will be invited to parties and functions where you suddenly become the center of attention. People respond to you positively, which feeds a growing feeling of well-being within you. You have more faith in yourself and your abilities.

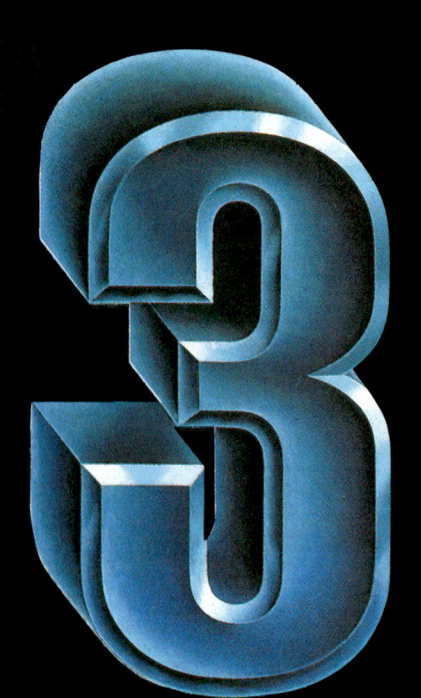

Essence of Four: Security. Four symbolizes the boundaries that provide security for the Three. As the square, the second perfect shape in mathematics, it suggests solid foundations and perimeters that contain and protect. The determined and conservative Four works hard to provide strong fences and square meals for the nourishment of the Three family.

Personal Number Four: You are practical, cautious, and reliable, the salt of the earth. You feel responsible for building solid foundations upon which the future depends. That is why you respect law and order. It also explains why your cupboard is never bare and you have something saved for that rainy day. You can be depended upon to be at the job every day and to finish any task assigned to you; you exemplify Kahlil Gibran's line from *The Prophet*, "Work is love made visible." You take pride in your work because it is an expression of yourself. You are concerned with the land and need to be connected in some manner, through a garden, nature trips, or environmental issues. Financial matters are of concern to you as well; they are another expression of the worth of your talents. You should avoid stubbornness, overwork, and hoarding.

Personal-Year-Cycle Four: The emphasis this year is on work, order, budgeting, foundations, close physical relationships, the body. You have an urge to organize all areas of your life, so you begin cleaning the attic, cellar, closets, the garage, the office. This action is a symbolic gesture indicative of your subconscious need to build an orderly and strong foundation in your life. Material things become important now because they add to your sense of security and satisfy your heightened physical needs. You may purchase goods or property, or decide to build or remodel. Exercise good judgment and organize your funds carefully. Your body is a physical possession, and since you may have put on a few pounds last year, now is the time to bring out the sweat suits, the diet book, and the bathroom scales. Health can be a concern, so rest, eat well, exercise properly, and have a physical examination. This can be a money cycle, but funds that come in are in direct proportion to the amount of work you do. Work well and you will be rewarded.

Essence of Five: Experience. Four, firmly entrenched in its home, now begins to explore the environment. The Five needs freedom and independence so that it can indulge its senses in the experiences of life. It has an insatiable curiosity through which it filters its encounters and ultimately makes choices that will influence its future.

Personal Number Five: You are a communicator. Impulsive and restless, you need the freedom to move freely through your life so that you can gather experience and information to feed your curiosity. You promote ideas and like change for the learning opportunity it provides. Mental stimulation is essential for your well-being. Your mind moves quickly, imitating and adapting to immediate influences so that you are able to blend in with any group. You can talk on most subjects with ease because of your vast experience, and you are a natural mimic, delighting others with your impish actions. Versatile and adaptable, you are the super salesperson and life of the party. You are efficient but dislike monotony and routine jobs. Because you have the power to communicate effectively, you should remain sincere and truthful.

Personal-Year-Cycle Five: You are restless and ready for change. Life suddenly becomes so busy that you feel as if you are on a merry-go-round, attending meetings and parties, running errands, answering mail and the telephone, and generally being available for others who suddenly need you. Communication is a key word this year. Get involved and meet people, because from these experiences you will gather the information you need to make important decisions that can affect your life for the next four years. If you are dissatisfied with your life, you can make changes more easily now. This is a turning point. Opportunities will arise in which you can find solutions to any current impasses. Because your mind is so active, this is a good time to take courses to satisfy your need for more experience. Your romantic desires increase, sending out magnetic waves that attract the opposite sex. Various love interests become possible. Your nervous system is in high gear, so avoid alcohol and drugs, and be careful of accidents. This is your year for fun, excitement, romantic encounters, decisions, and change.

Essence of Six: Harmony. After tasting experience through its five senses, Six realizes the importance of love, compassion, and social responsibility. The home, built in the Four, must now be filled with love and meaningful relationships. Home also becomes part of the community in which law and order are established to ensure social harmony.

Personal Number Six: You are an artistic individual whose sense of harmony may express itself in the home, the arts, or community service. You need and show love in your home, where family is all-important. Your sense of beauty may be evident in the way you decorate your home, or in crafts and cooking. Your innate ability to go right to the crux of the matter makes you the counselor to whom others go for answers to their problems as well as for the nurturing compassion you provide. If your profession is outside the home, you seek to bring harmonious order to the world through beautifying the environment, counseling, the arts, or through the legal system, which seeks balance in justice. You love people and are concerned, generous, and tolerant. Be careful to avoid becoming a recluse or a doormat for others, playing the martyr.

Personal-Year-Cycle Six: This is the nesting phase where the emphasis is on home and family. In the natural order of things, after last year's possible romantic encounters, marriage and the birth of children are possible. Even if this does not apply to you, your attention shifts to the domestic front, and changes occur, such as family members moving in or out, children going to school or marrying, relatives wanting financial or emotional support. Responsibility for the family increases. Because your sense of justice is heightened, people may tell you their problems and ask your advice. Court decisions that restore balance are possible. Beauty and harmony become important in your life, so you may redecorate your home, surround yourself with works of art, and enjoy attending museums or the ballet. Community projects can satisfy your social sensibilities now. And close relationships with your partner, family, and friends are possible if you extend love and compassion.

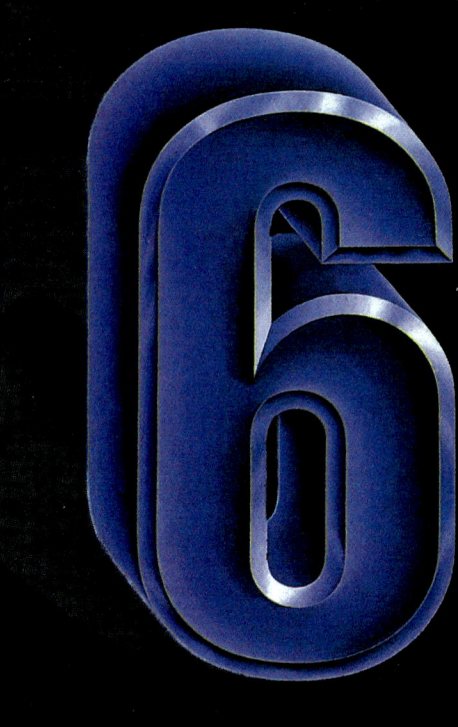

Essence of Seven: Analysis. Now that the physical is taken care of, Seven goes within itself to contemplate its place in the universe. It begins to think and to analyze past experiences and present situations, and it wonders what lies ahead. Seven realizes that the skills it has developed must be perfected in preparation for the future. Seven is physical rest and mental work.

Personal Number Seven: You are a thinker and an idealist who thoroughly analyzes knowledge from many sources before accepting any premises. Noises and crowds disrupt your meditative nature; therefore, you spend time by yourself so your creative imagination can roam freely seeking perfection. Your intuitive abilities combined with your naturally analytic nature make you a prophet, able to anticipate future needs and events. You understand human nature and are not easily fooled by external appearances, and thus can make others uneasy. Because of your introspective demeanor, you are a puzzle to many. As a rule, you will not accept orthodox beliefs but will search for your own—although you may find these within the walls of conventional educational or spiritual institutions. Try to listen to other ideas and do not allow your naturally aloof manner to alienate you from those you love.

Personal-Year-Cycle Seven: It is time to rest. You feel more tired and less social than usual and want to be alone to think about where you have been, where you are now, where you are headed. You may spend time with one or two friends who complement your contemplative mood. This cycle says it is time to go within and think. You have to maintain your everyday routine to some extent, but do not push your affairs aggressively—if you persist in scurrying about in the outside world, you may become ill. You can set your material worries aside; the things you have been worrying about for the past six years will take care of themselves. Your mind is keenly alert, and you should perfect any skills that you have; they will be useful next year. But for now, study, read, and take courses in philosophy, religion, numerology, astrology, or other metaphysical subjects to help you understand your place in life. Your intuitions are keen, and dreams, visions, and telepathic experiences are all possible.

Essence of Eight: Reward. The strength and skills gathered in the past seven numbers are now put to the test. Well grounded physically, emotionally, and mentally, the Eight reaches out into the world to establish its authority in positions of material power. The rewards for its past efforts come in equal proportion to the wisdom of past choices. This is the karmic period where Eight reaps what it has sown.

Personal Number Eight: You are the executive type in whichever sphere you move. Sensing your organizational and managerial abilities, people automatically look to you for leadershp. You know the value of a dollar, so your sound fiscal judgment can place you in positions of financial management. By working hard and exercising discipline and caution, you can achieve positions of great power. You do not rely on luck; you depend upon your own resourcefulness and perseverance. You know no halfway measures; your ambition drives you to achieve success. You must accept responsibility and handle it fairly because your actions have obvious repercussions in the world around you. As a steward of material resources, you must handle them wisely and with respect. Scheming and ruthless actions and personal advancement without regard for others lead to defeat.

Personal-Year-Cycle Eight: This year you will get what you have earned. Pursue your career goals with confidence and determination, because now you will be noticed. If you have planned well, you will get that promotion, raise, or recognition. Honors, awards, and legacies are also possible. You are finding out how effective you are in the material world. It is a year of pressure and responsibility in career and in finances. Depending upon your past actions, the reins of power can be placed in your hands—and possibly large sums of money. Personal relationships are also intense. To fulfill the needs of this cycle—as opposed to your Five Cycle, where romantic activities were for the purpose of experience—your relationships now must embody respect and equality, the physical and the spiritual, body and mind. You can find wholeness here, but whatever this cycle presents to you, an examination of your behavior during the past seven cycles will reveal how you arrived at this point.

Essence of Nine: Release. After experiencing the world of material power in the Eight, Nine now knows that physical things are transitory and must be returned to the giver. Having learned that life is cyclical, Nine gives back freely and without fear those things it has gained so that the universe will be richer. Nine is the humanitarian carrying the light of wisdom.

Personal Number Nine: You are the humanitarian who feels compassion and love for others regardless of social, economic, or racial barriers. Because you understand that you are part of a greater whole, you give generously of your time and resources. You seek wisdom rather than mere knowledge, desiring to make the world a more loving place in which to live. Because you belong to the universal family, you know that you have to live impersonally and let go of things when it is time. People are drawn to you because of your tolerance, inner wisdom, and breadth of vision, which is often prophetic. You must live your own philosophy because you are an example for others. The necessities of life may come easily so that you are free to follow your humanitarian impulses. Avoid self-serving interests, which can only lead to a lack of faith in life's bounty.

Personal-Year-Cycle Nine: This is the final year in your nine-year cycle, a cleansing period in which those things no longer necessary in your life must be discarded to make room for a new round of experience in next year's Personal-Year-Cycle One. Major changes occur now. People may leave your life, you may change jobs or have to relocate, and things you have grown used to may have to be given up. Your attitude changes dramatically. Use some of your energy in charitable deeds. Give back to life some of what you have been given so that you can experience firsthand the joy of giving. These acts are integral to the transition process. Old friendships become especially meaningful now; new ones can develop. You may receive gifts for your past efforts. Many goals have been accomplished, and you should tie up loose ends. The past eight years have added to your pool of wisdom. Sprinkle others with your sympathy, compassion, and understanding, and be open to the cleansing wash of change. An exciting new year lies ahead, beginning with your next birthday.

Casting Your Fate

"The die is cast," said Shakespeare's Julius Caesar as he crossed the Rubicon in the great gamble of his career. The expression was new, but the linkage of dice and destiny was a very ancient idea.

Forerunners of dice, made of bone, probably existed tens of thousands of years ago. They were almost surely used for gambling and quite likely for fortune-telling as well. It appears that primitive man concocted divinatory games as avenues through which gods could send omens concerning the future.

Among the first dice, much used by the Greeks and Romans but far older, were those carved from the four-sided knucklebones of sheep. They were called astragali. The decorations on their faces, though not necessarily dots, had designated values for use in gaming and augury. For centuries, astragali existed alongside cube dice bearing the pattern they have today—the spots on opposite sides always totaling seven. These came into use around 1400 BC.

Other dice existed in Egypt at least as early as 3500 BC. How they served for divination is lost to history, but certain gambling uses are clear. Excavations of Egyptian tombs have turned up loaded dice, made specifically for cheating.

Several methods of telling your fortune with dice have evolved over the years. Unlike numerology, the *I Ching*, or the Tarot, they require little expertise and so are easy to try at home.

Perhaps the simplest system involves questions and answers. You invent the questions, depending on what you want to know. Will I be married soon? could be asked, or Will I be rich? or Should I change jobs at this time? Then devise a list of possible answers, numbered from four to twenty-four. Some examples are: Yes, definitely, Yes, if you work hard, Not at this time, or Only if you persist. With a particular question in mind, throw two dice and add their numbers. Then throw again and add the second total to the first. With that result, consult your answers list for the corresponding response to your question. More formal methods require a little ritual preparation and—according to tradition—attention to circumstances. Friday and Sunday are said to be unauspicious for divination. Cool weather is considered best for dice casting, and a tranquil atmosphere is essential. Be absolutely silent as you throw the dice.

Draw a circle about a foot in diameter and put it on a table or some other flat surface. This will be your target in throwing, and you must take care to hit it. To have the dice fall outside the circle or on the floor is unlucky. Use three dice. If all three of the dice land outside the circle on your first cast, try again. If this happens once more, the time is not auspicious, and you should abandon the experiment for the present.

The total face value of the three dice in one throw yields the number for a divinatory message, such as those found in the following list derived from traditional sources:

Three. Unexpected good news, a

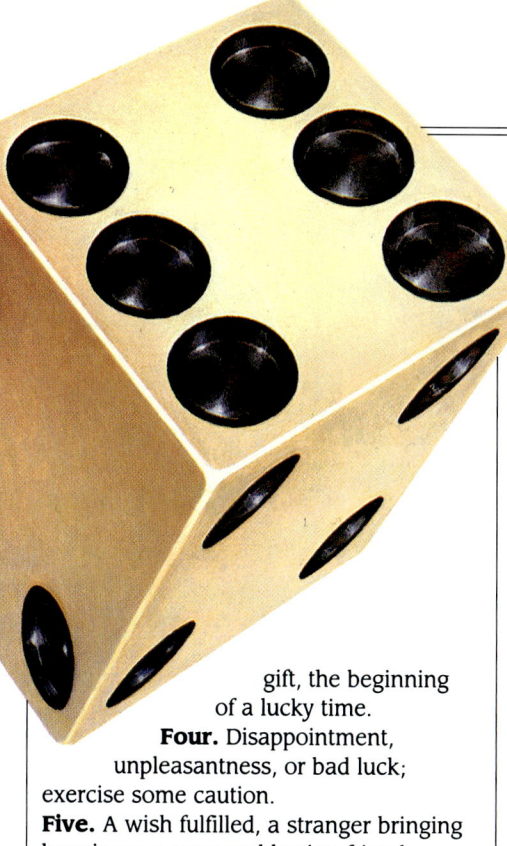

gift, the beginning of a lucky time.
Four. Disappointment, unpleasantness, or bad luck; exercise some caution.
Five. A wish fulfilled, a stranger bringing happiness, a new and lasting friend.
Six. Financial loss, dishonest friends or loved ones.
Seven. Setbacks, unhappiness, scandal or gossip; guard your secrets.
Eight. Strong outside forces; blame, fair or unfair, headed your way.
Nine. Luck in love or in marriage, reconciliation, a wedding or some other kind of festivity.
Ten. A birth, domestic happiness; a business promotion.
Eleven. A parting, possible illness, unhappiness for you or someone close.
Twelve. Good news, maybe by letter or telephone, but get advice before replying.
Thirteen. Grief and sorrow, depression and worry.
Fourteen. Help from a friend, a new friend or admirer.
Fifteen. Caution—guard against temptation toward dishonesty, avoid arguments and gossip.
Sixteen. Travel, a good journey.
Seventeen. A change caused by someone from afar, a move, cheerful industriousness.
Eighteen. The luckiest number of all, boding success, wealth, advancement, and happiness.

For more specific revelations about your future, a third method may yield more complete meanings. Divide your circle into twelve equal parts and assign letters to each one. Each section will pertain to a particular aspect of your life, as follows:

A The next year
B Finances
C Travel
D Domestic affairs
E The present
F Health
G Love and marriage
H Legal matters
I Your current emotional state
J Career
K Friends
L Enemies

Again, use three dice. But with this system, the dice are not totaled after they are thrown. Rather, the number that turns up on the die landing in a particular segment is the one to conjure with. Thus you are dealing only with numbers one through six. Their meanings are as follows:

One. Favorable aspects, but they should be related to the reading as a whole.
Two. Success depends on your friends.
Three. Signs are excellent for success.
Four. Disappointment and difficulties.
Five. Auspicious indications.
Six. Uncertainty.

Say, for example, you throw your three dice and turn up a four on letter *F*, a six on *E*, and a two on *A*. The *F*/four combination might mean health problems are in the offing, and therefore a medical checkup could be advisable. The *E*/six takes up the theme, indicating a degree of uncertainty in your life at the moment. Combining the two divinations, you might conclude that less than optimum health at the present time is the cause of doubt and unease. But the *A*/two augurs a favorable outcome, indicating that the year to come will bring good things, provided you take care to get along with people.

Like most divination systems, dice casting permits—even encourages—you to read your own meanings into the fall of the cubes. And, as is generally the case with augury, there is no empirical evidence whatever to prove the dice are accurate. Yet tales of truth-telling dice do exist, as one might expect with a divinatory system that predates history itself.

Dominoes and Destiny

While nowhere near as old as dice, dominoes are nevertheless respectably antique. The first record of them comes from twelfth-century China, where they were probably used for divination rather than gaming. In fact, some antiquarians believe dominoes evolved as an early form of dice, a variety that was employed exclusively for occult practices.

They are still widely used for fortune-telling in Korea and India; and in both India and China there are domino games that combine gambling and augury. Certain tiles are thought to be lucky for a player, regardless of the outcome of the game.

Dominoes apparently made their way to Europe by way of China, and in the West the tiles took on their current name and a more modern form. By the end of the eighteenth century, they were in use in Italy, France, and England. They probably were named after a black-and-white masquerade costume called the domino—popular in Europe at the time—that matched the color combination of the common ebony-and-ivory tiles.

Modern dominoes are usually made of wood, ivory, or plastic. Standard sets in the West consist of twenty-eight rectangular tiles, one of them completely blank and the others marked on one side with dots. Each tile is bisected, and the halves that are not blank bear dots numbering one to six. Thus they represent all of the possible number combinations, ranging from double blank to double six.

In their occidental incarnation, dominoes have tended to be far more popular as a game than as a tool for divination. Even so, Western methods for telling fortunes with them have evolved over the centuries and still persist.

To begin your domino reading, place all the tiles face down and then shuffle them. Three tiles will be used for the reading, and they may be selected in either of two ways. You may pick all three at once, or you may choose them one at a time, reading the chosen domino and divining its message and then returning it to the pile to be shuffled again. The second method offers the possibility that the same tile could be drawn twice. If this happens, an immediate fulfillment of the message is indicated.

However the tiles are drawn, only three may be used at a sitting. Moreover, it is said that you should not divine with dominoes more than once a week, lest the results lose all meaning.

Here are the traditional meanings of the various number combinations to be found on a single tile:

Six/six. The luckiest domino of them all, forecasting happiness, success, and prosperity in all aspects of life.
Six/five. Enhanced status, the presence of a close friend or patron, a sign that any kindness will bring you esteem, a caution toward patience and tenacity.
Six/four. A quarrel, perhaps even an unsuccessful lawsuit.
Six/three. Travel, enjoyment, a happy holiday; a gift.
Six/two. Good luck and improved circumstances but only for those who are honest.
Six/one. A wedding; an end to problems, possibly as a result of the intervention of a good friend.
Six/blank. Beware of false friends, for their malicious gossip could cause suffering for you.
Five/five. Change bringing success, a beneficial move, money that results from a new idea.
Five/four. Financial luck, possibly unexpected, but avoid making investments at this time.
Five/three. Calm, serenity; a guest; good news or helpful advice given to you by your boss or a visitor.
Five/two. Birth, influence from a true and patient friend, sociability and enjoyment.
Five/one. A love affair or new friend, possible unhappy endings for those who are in love.
Five/blank. Sadness, the necessity of comforting a friend in trouble but with tact and caution.
Four/four. Happiness, celebration, relaxation, fun.
Four/three. Happiness and success instead of expected disappointments but possible domestic problems.
Four/two. An unhappy change, setbacks, loss, possibly a theft. Beware of a deceitful acquaintance.
Four/one. Financial problems ahead, pay outstanding debts.
Four/blank. Bad news; disappointment in love, temporarily thwarted goals. Reconcile disagreements.
Three/three. Emotional obstacles, jealousy, but beneficial financial indications; a wedding.

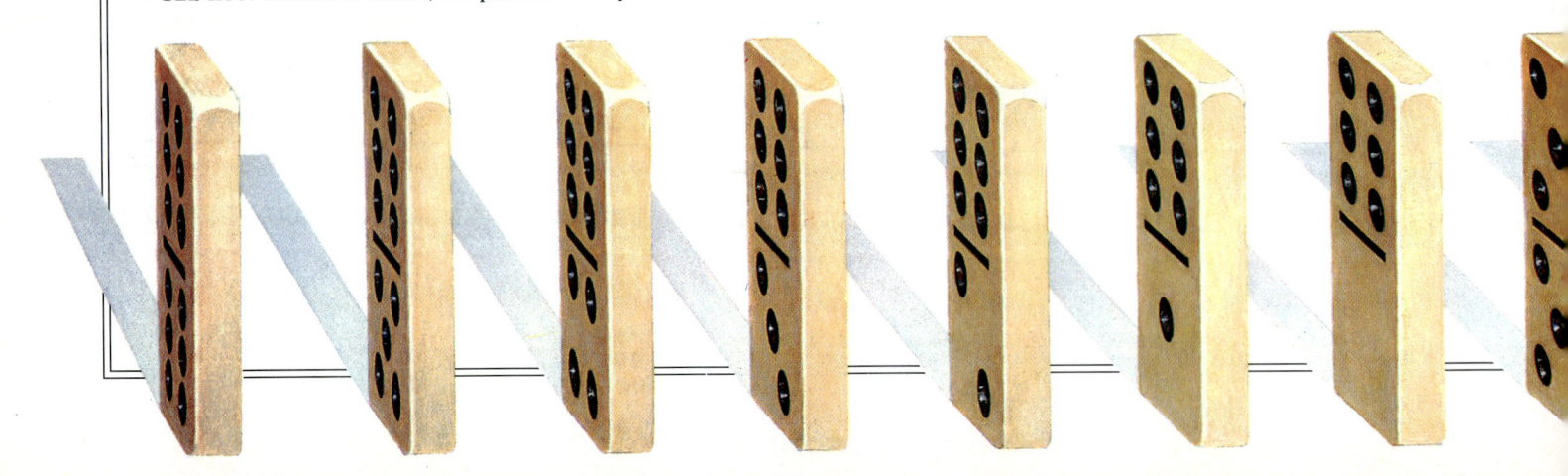

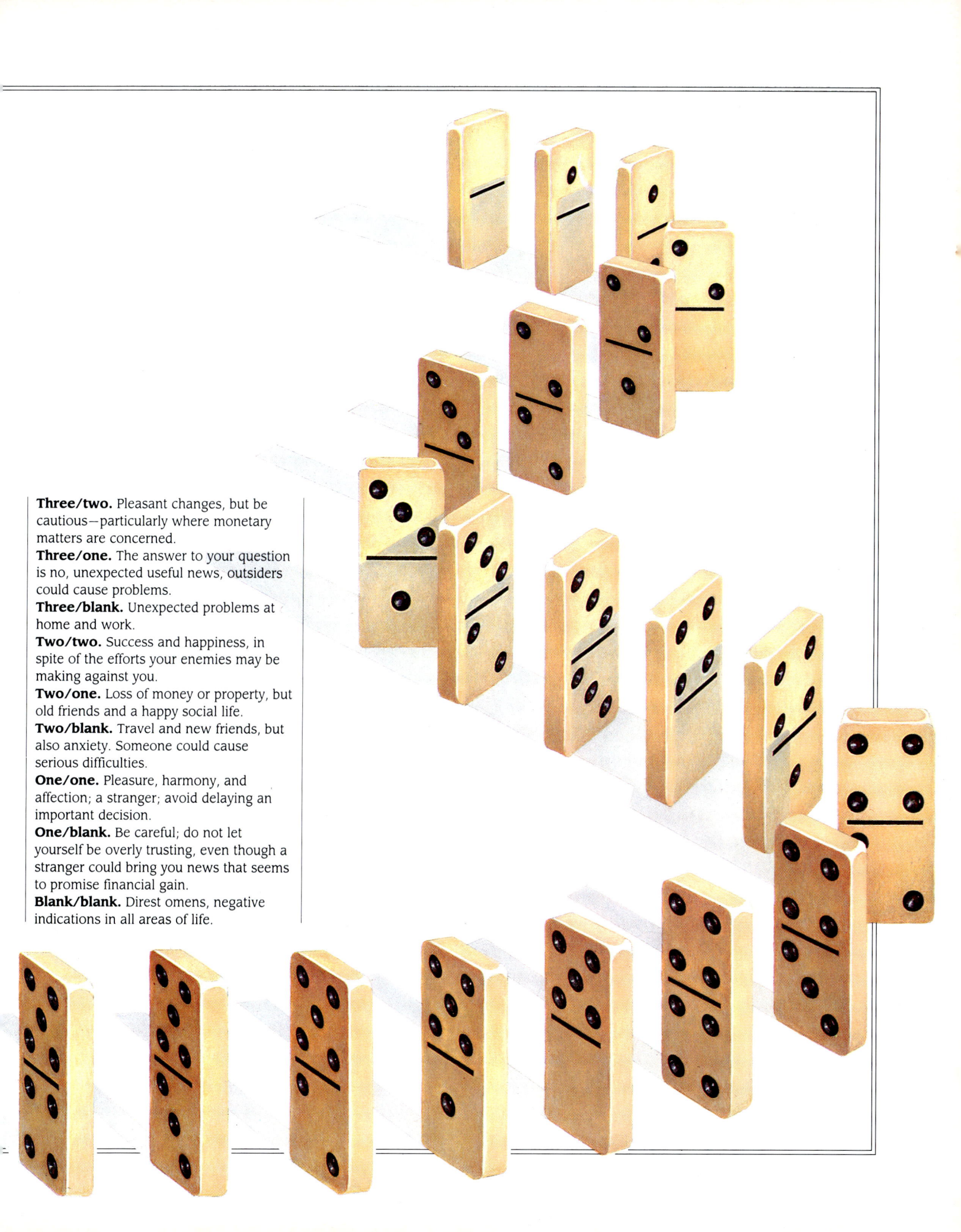

Three/two. Pleasant changes, but be cautious—particularly where monetary matters are concerned.
Three/one. The answer to your question is no, unexpected useful news, outsiders could cause problems.
Three/blank. Unexpected problems at home and work.
Two/two. Success and happiness, in spite of the efforts your enemies may be making against you.
Two/one. Loss of money or property, but old friends and a happy social life.
Two/blank. Travel and new friends, but also anxiety. Someone could cause serious difficulties.
One/one. Pleasure, harmony, and affection; a stranger; avoid delaying an important decision.
One/blank. Be careful; do not let yourself be overly trusting, even though a stranger could bring you news that seems to promise financial gain.
Blank/blank. Direst omens, negative indications in all areas of life.

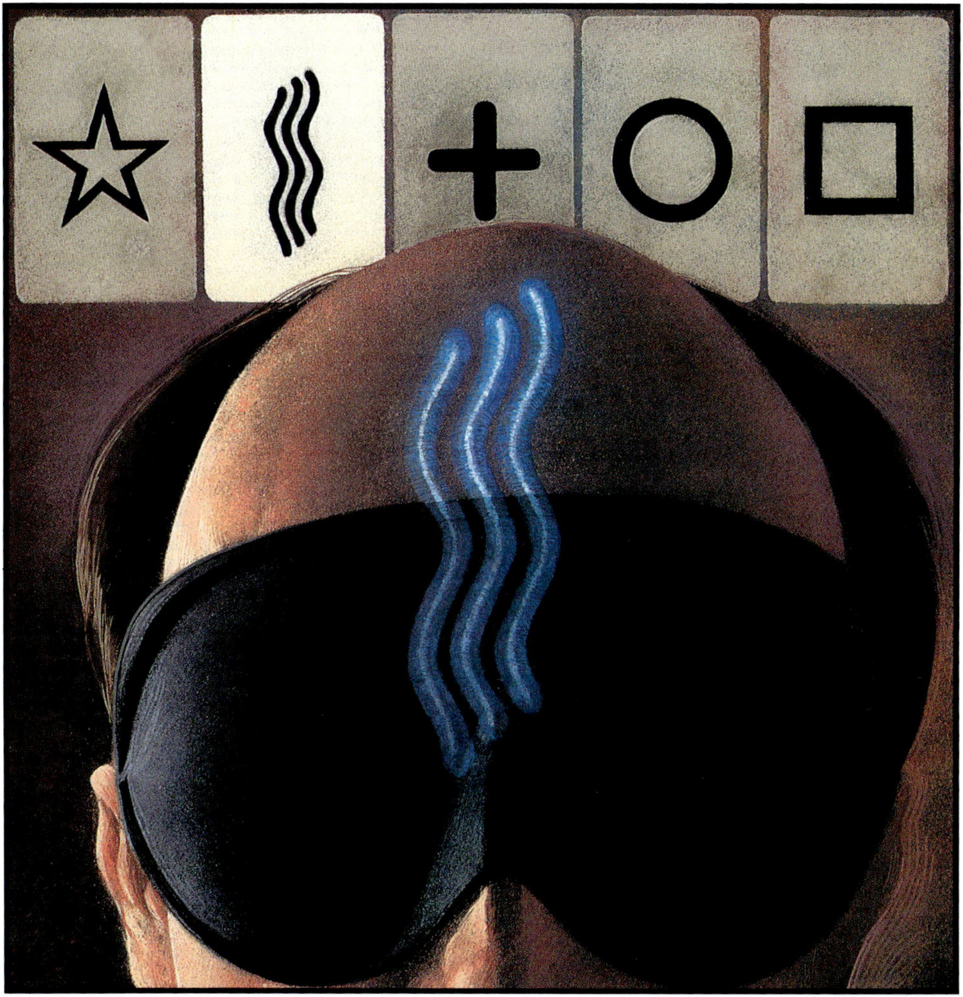

A Fire that Raged in a Mind's Eye

On the evening of July 9, 1759, a pleasant party was just beginning at the home of a prominent citizen of Goteborg, Sweden. Suddenly, unaccountably, the most eminent of the sixteen guests—the famed scientist and mystic Emanuel Swedenborg—left and walked outside without explanation. When he returned a short time later, he was pale and shaken. A fire was raging, he said. It had already destroyed a friend's house and now threatened his own.

The guests exchanged startled glances. As they all knew, Swedenborg did not live in Goteborg, but in Stockholm. And Stockholm was almost three hundred miles away.

The party proceeded, but Swedenborg left the house several more times and returned to report the blaze was still spreading. Finally, at 8:00 P.M., he announced that it had been extinguished—only three houses from his own.

By the next morning, a Sunday, Swedenborg's vision was the talk of Goteborg. Had there really been a fire? Or was the seventy-one-year-old's imagination running amok? An apparent answer came the following night when an express messenger arrived from Stockholm with news of a great fire. Three days after the vision, a second messenger brought more details. They matched Swedenborg's account of the blaze and confirmed that it had halted only three doors from his own and had ended, just as he said, at 8:00 P.M.

Swedenborg was a respected engineer, inventor, and author whose intellect encompassed sciences ranging from psychology to zoology. When he was in his late fifties, however, he received what he regarded as a visitation from God. Thereafter, he turned his full attention to theology, metaphysics, and the exploration of his psychic powers, which seemed abundant.

To many parapsychologists, Swedenborg's reported vision of the Stockholm fire is an example of clairvoyance: the ability to see psychically what the eye cannot perceive.

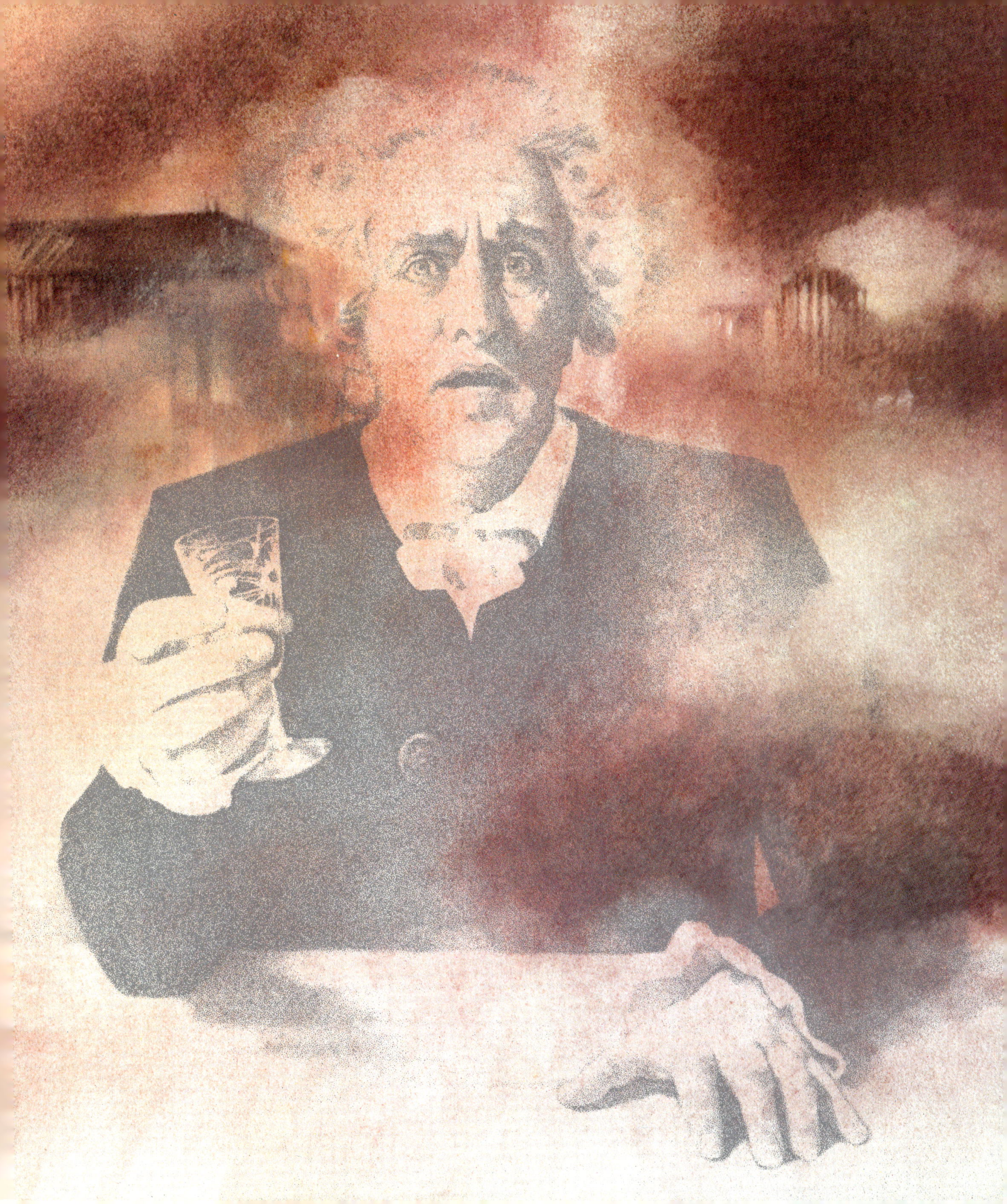

When Past Met Present on a Country Road

Dr. Edward Gibson Moon, a country physician in England, considered himself a hardheaded man of science, but an experience he had in the early 1930s shook his faith in orthodox notions of time.

One of Moon's patients was Lord Edward Carson, who lived on the Isle of Thanet. The front steps of his house, Cleve Court, led to a semicircular driveway that opened at either end onto a country lane. A tall hedge screened the house from the road.

Lord Carson was very ill, and Moon saw him daily. After one morning's visit, the physician stood at the head of the steps, deep in thought about his patient. As he told the story later, he was not much mindful of his surroundings when he happened to glance up toward the hedge.

But there was no hedge. Nor did a road lie beyond where the hedge should have been. Try as he might, Moon could not see a single familiar landmark. There was only a muddy track stretching across empty fields. Odder still was the man walking up the track toward the house. He carried a flintlock and was wearing breeches, riding boots, a caped overcoat, and a top hat with a narrow crown—haberdashery long out of fashion—and he appeared to belong in another century, perhaps the late eighteenth or early nineteenth.

To Moon it seemed the stranger saw him as well. The visitor stopped midstride, and for a moment the two men gaped at each other. Trying to orient himself, Moon turned to see whether Cleve Court was still behind him. It was, and when he turned again he found the landscape had righted itself. The hedge and the road were in their accustomed places, and the stranger had vanished.

Some parapsychologists interpret the doctor's vision as an instance of simultaneous retrocognition and precognition. Through a tear in the fabric of time, Moon was peering into the past—retrocognition. The stranger, if indeed he saw the doctor, experienced precognition—seeing the future.

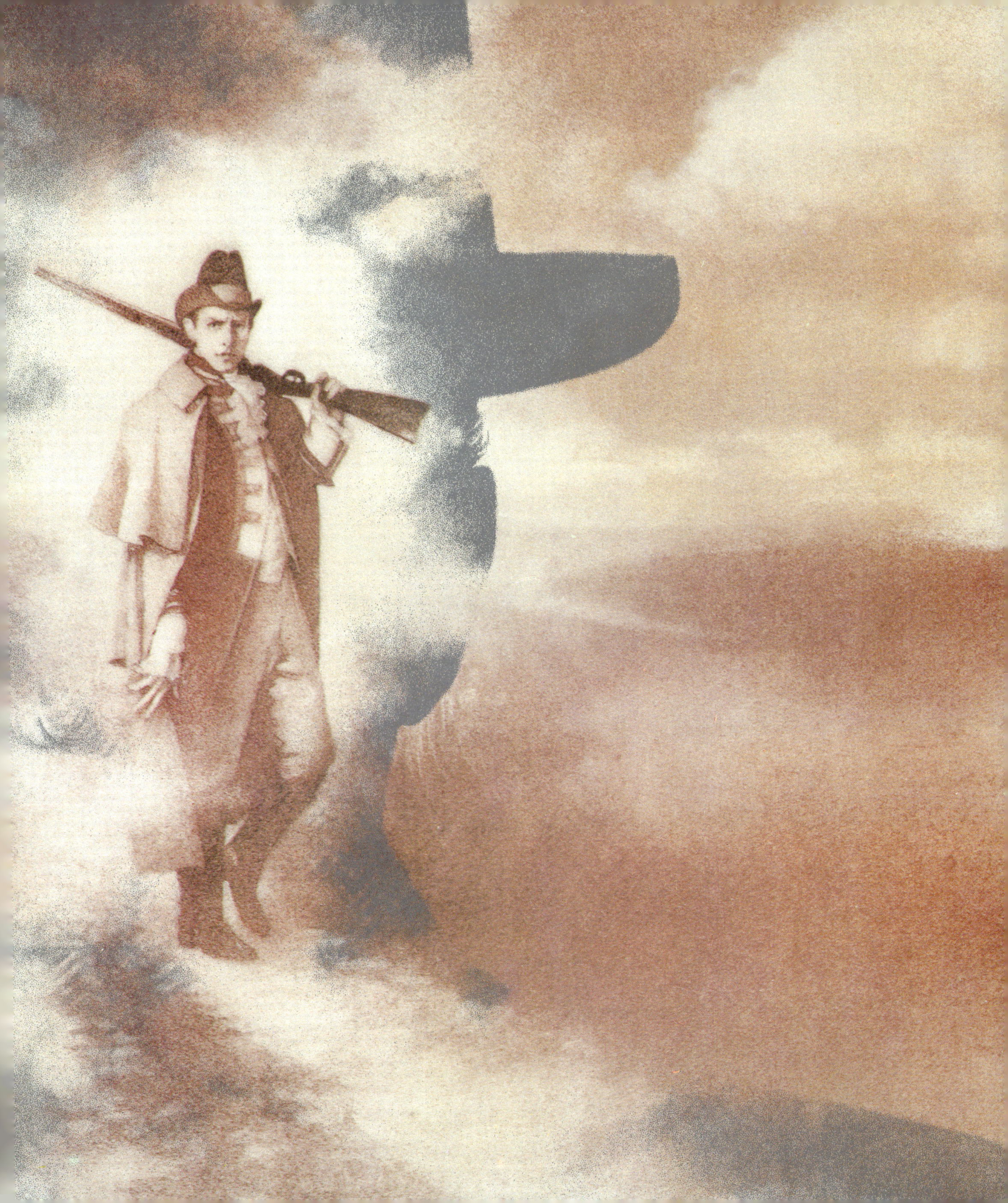

An Apprehension of Danger

One day in 1955, five-year-old Joicey Hurth of Cedarburg, Wisconsin, came home from a birthday party to find that her father and two brothers had gone to a movie without her. The theater was only a block and a half away, so the little girl dashed out to join them.

Shortly after the child left, her mother, also named Joicey, was washing dishes at the kitchen sink when suddenly, inexplicably, she knew her daughter had been in an accident. Without hesitation, Mrs. Joicey Hurth ran to the telephone and dialed the theater.

"My little girl was on the way to the theater," she told the woman who answered. "She has had an accident. Is she badly hurt?"

"How did you know?" stammered the confused theater employee. "It—the accident—just happened."

Indeed, it turned out that the child, in rushing to join her father and brothers, had run into the path of a moving car just outside the movie house. After being hit, she had bounced off a fender and landed on the pavement, but she was not badly hurt.

"I did not see or have a mental image of a car hitting Joicey," the mother recalled, "but I did have the impression so strongly that I did not question it or hesitate to call the theater."

Recounting the episode some years later, the daughter said that just after she was hit by the car she ran to the side of the street, crying and calling out in her mind, "Mama, Mama, Mama!" She was, she believed, "screaming inaudibly."

Since Mrs. Hurth neither heard nor saw anything that could have alerted her to her daughter's mishap, parapsychologists studying the case attributed her knowledge of it to telepathy—direct mind-to-mind communication occurring without the five senses.

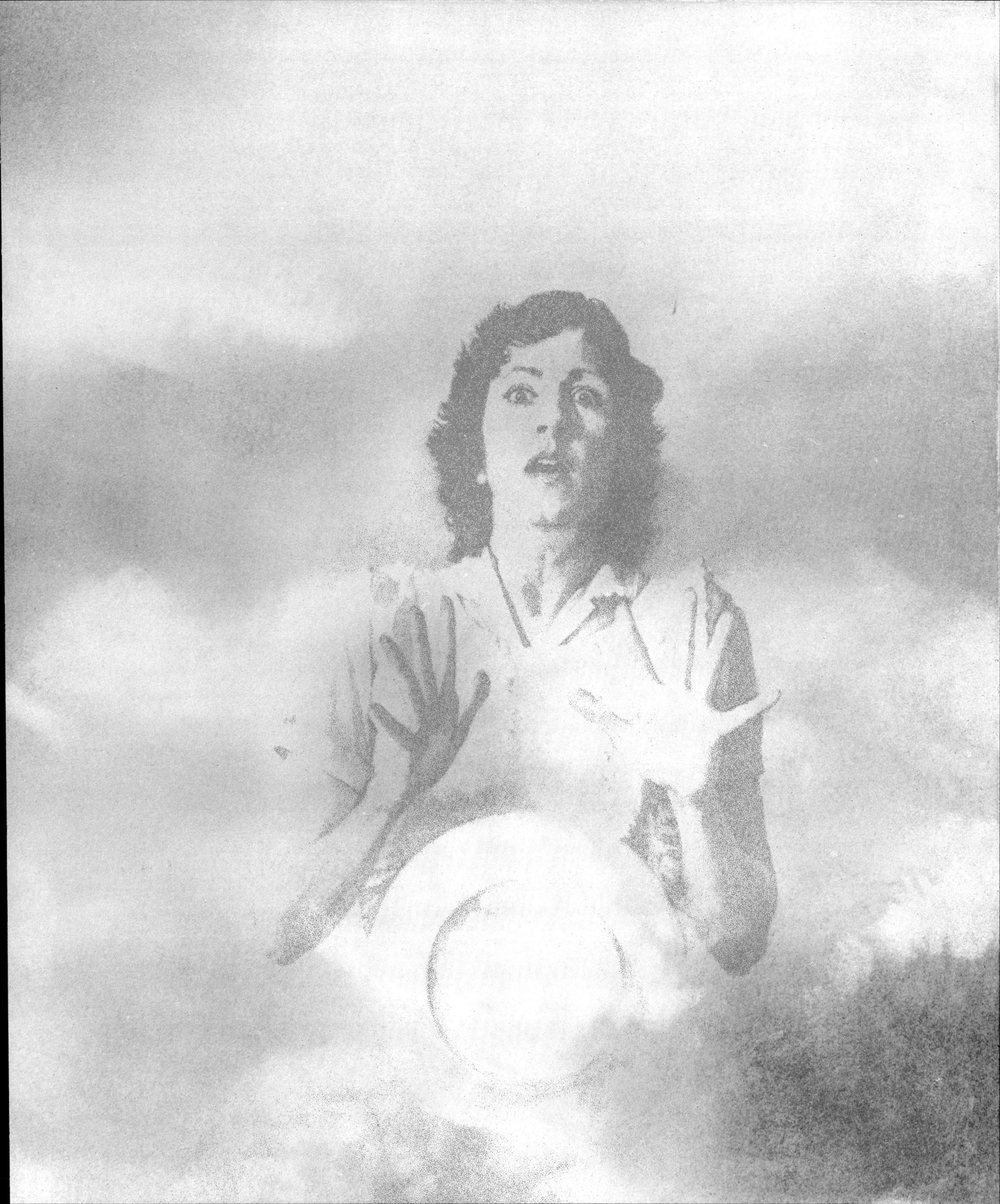

In a dream of his own death, Abraham Lincoln stood at the foot of a coffin in the White House and saw a shrouded corpse. When

he asked who had died, a soldier among the shadowy mourners answered: "The president. He was killed by an assassin."

The World of the Psychic

The room was all white except for dark brown wainscoting around its bottom half. A strong, astringent smell hung in the air, an odor that meant hospital to the small boy strapped onto the hard white table. Two-year-old Ingo Swann was about to undergo what the grownups called a tonsillectomy. He understood that the operation was necessary to make his throat stop hurting, but he also understood that he was afraid. Struggling against the restraining straps and caterwauling with all his might, he resisted the nurse's effort to cover his face with a dark mask. She retreated, only to return with a half-filled balloon.

"I bet you can't blow this up further," she teased. The air in the balloon smelled funny, but young Ingo took up the challenge. In moments, the room's bright lights began to fade and dim. Then—Ingo Swann would write long afterward—a strange thing happened. The white walls turned emerald, and the dark wainscoting took on an iridescent glow. Ingo felt himself hovering about three feet above his own body, secure in the shadows above the glare of the table, watching the surgery in progress. He gazed down at the doctor and the nurse and his mother, who had been allowed into the operating room to help calm him. He watched the scalpel slip and nick the back of his own tongue, and he heard the doctor curse in response. He watched the nurse put two small, brown objects—presumably his tonsils—into a bottle and stow them behind some rolls of tissue on a table against the wall.

Some time later, when Ingo came out from under the ether, he demanded to be given his tonsils.

"Now, now," the nurse said to the little boy, "We have already thrown those dirty things away."

"No you didn't," the child snapped, pointing toward the rolls of paper. "You put them behind those over there."

The doctor, the nurse, and his mother exchanged alarmed glances. Nobody spoke. The nurse had done exactly as Ingo said: The tonsils were in the bottle behind the rolls of paper on the table. The grownups could not understand how he could know—and he could not understand why he should not know. He often had the sensation of seeming to leave his own body and watching from a distance what was happening around it. But he had not yet learned that the experience, although known to psychics by a number of names—out-of-body experiences and astral travel among them—was not in the ken of most people.

Swann would grow up to become a noted psychic artist, his canvases filled with auric light he presumably saw emanating from the life he painted. For a time, discouraged by the cultural mind-set that viewed his claimed psychic powers as impossible, he stopped cultivating them. He eventually renewed an active interest, however, prompted partly by plants and animals. He noticed that he seemed to communicate telepathically with his pet chinchilla, which would exhibit great distress if Swann merely thought of putting it into its cage for the night. In addition, he felt he was able to receive mental signals from a bedraggled *Dracaena massangeana*—a common house plant. For example, Swann believed he could pick up on the plant's "mental" complaints of being watered too much or of lacking proper minerals in its soil.

Concluding to his own satisfaction that something noteworthy was going on, he submitted to testing by some of parapsychology's leading researchers. The results were often extraordinary. At the American Society for Psychical Research, for instance, he purportedly proved adept at remote viewing *(opposite)*, and in experiments with Dr. Gertrude R. Schmeidler of the City University of New York, he demonstrated apparent psychokinesis—the ability to alter the physical environment, such as changing the air temperature inside sealed vacuum bottles, through mind power alone.

Still, his frustrations persisted. Although Swann greatly admired the work of Schmeidler and never abandoned psychic experimentation, he found much of it disillusioning. He concluded that science was too often wanting imagination and strictured by its own rationalist traditions, and that it was not yet up to the intricate task of exploring the world of the psychic. In the main, Swann said, researchers had "only succeeded in grinding the diamond into a dust pile while trying to capture the sparkle."

Yet, even as Swann wrote those words in a memoir published in 1975, the psychic world was exploding from the confines of the laboratory, where it had migrated from séance rooms and side shows only a few decades before. Blending with the neomysticism and antimaterialism of the 1960s and the self-realization movement of the 1970s, a pursuit of things psychic had at last infiltrated the mainstream of twentieth-century culture. Psychic powers were part of a loose amalgam that, in the years after Swann described his experiences, came under the general title the New Age. It was an age in which old definitions were expanded and blurred. Telepathy, clairvoyance, precognition, and retrocognition were all part of the New Age paraphernalia, but these aspects by no means circumscribed the movement. Whatever its tools, its goals were so-called higher consciousness, enlightened awareness.

New groups and movements arose to help psi enthusiasts escape the mundane world in ways ranging from simple meditation to astral voyaging and pagan rituals. Some aspirants to enlightenment flocked to so-called channelers, people who transmit purported sublime truths from spirits long dead. Others looked to psychic advisers to counsel them on their present lives, predict their futures, or even regress them through past existences.

Ingo Swann, who apparently possessed psi talents that most New Agers could merely aspire to, had little patience with the movement's mystical trappings. Believing the psychic impulse was of a piece with the creative urge in the human psyche and was in no way paranormal, he thought weird mysticism as great a trap as smug rationalism to those seeking a wider awareness of the universe. "Granted many individuals, their synapses misfiring or their alleged karma catching up with them, do sometimes go bonkers and create confusion among their fellow men," Swann wrote. "But, even so, this is no sign that all people whose imagination and consciousness wander beyond the immediate barriers of ideas of consciousness are bonkers."

Many detractors were less restrained in their contempt for New Age doings. Most traditional religionists warned against the psychic boom as idolatry. ESP skeptics insisted that years of scientific research had produced, at best, only the flimsiest evidence that psychic phenomena existed in any form. The ubiquitous New Agers, however, believed otherwise. No longer the province of academics on the one hand or the lunatic fringe on the other, the world of the psychic had become respectable, even fashionable in a way. And it was quite densely populated.

While the New Age was spawned partially by broad cultural trends that directly preceded it, it was not without its individual progenitors. In particular, it owed a debt to two recent giants of psychism: Eileen Garrett and Edgar Cayce. They operated quite differently, but each seemed able—while unconscious—to gain access to information not available to the waking mind. Garrett functioned mostly as a medium—a conduit for spirits of the dead. Cayce was renowned as a psychic healer and a prophet. Firm conclusions about the nature of their apparent powers eluded both of these two people, though others theorized that clairvoyance, or telepathy, or both, figured in their work.

Garrett was born Eileen Jeanette Vancho in mist-shrouded County Meath in Ireland. She spent her childhood near the mystical Hill of Tara, a fey countryside where, she said later, "the 'little people' were universally accepted as an everyday part of normal existence." This myth-laden landscape was one of two factors she credited for the possible origin of her psychic gifts. The other was what she called "the almost equally universal acceptance of death as an intimate element of the daily round." She granted the possibility that the dead could communicate with the living and was fairly comfortable serving as a vehicle for the dialogue.

Certainly, death was an intimate specter in Garrett's personal life. Both her parents committed suicide while she was still an infant; one of her three husbands was killed in World War I, and only one of her four children survived into adulthood. But for all the death surrounding her, Garrett was anything but morbid.

"She hated to be deprived of any experience within her grasp—or even slightly beyond it," Garrett's daughter, Eileen Coley, has said. "She was such an entertaining personality—interested in so many things, so many people. If I could be fascinated by waking up at 7 A.M. to exchange funny stories with her, you can imagine what sort of person she was. A lot of people likened her to Auntie Mame." Indeed, according to Coley, novelist Patrick Dennis knew Garrett and used her as a prototype for his zany, globe-trotting heroine in *Auntie Mame*. It was Garrett's sheer force of personality, at least as much as

The Vision of Ingo Swann

Remote viewing—seeing beyond the range of physical vision—is one of several psychic talents attributed to Ingo Swann. To test his abilities, the American Society for Psychical Research devised an experiment in 1972. Pictures or objects were placed on a suspended platform; seated below it, pad and pencil in hand, Swann tried to see the images and then draw them while electrodes measured his brain's electrical activity *(above)*.

The substantially accurate sketches shown here, detailing shapes and colors of two abstract pictures on the platform, were among his successes. Swann believed he saw the objects by traveling out of his body, floating upward to where the pictures lay. Other possibilities considered by ASPR researchers are clairvoyance—having a vision of the pictures—or telepathy, reading the mind of someone who knew the platform's contents.

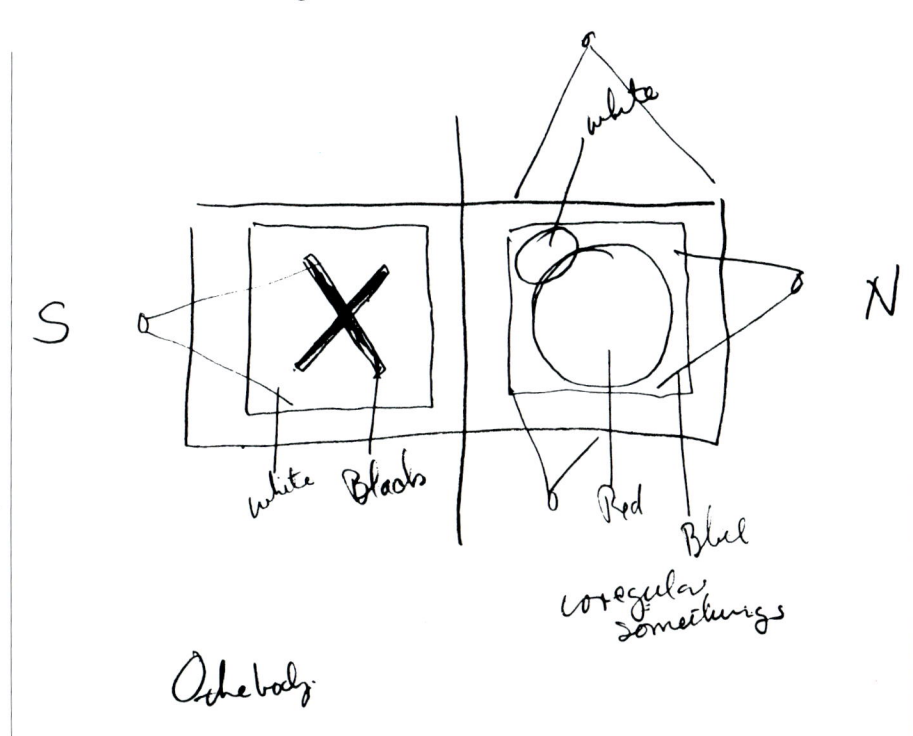

her alleged psychic gifts, that made such an impact on the many people she influenced.

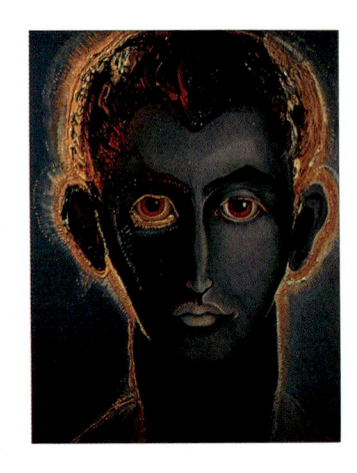

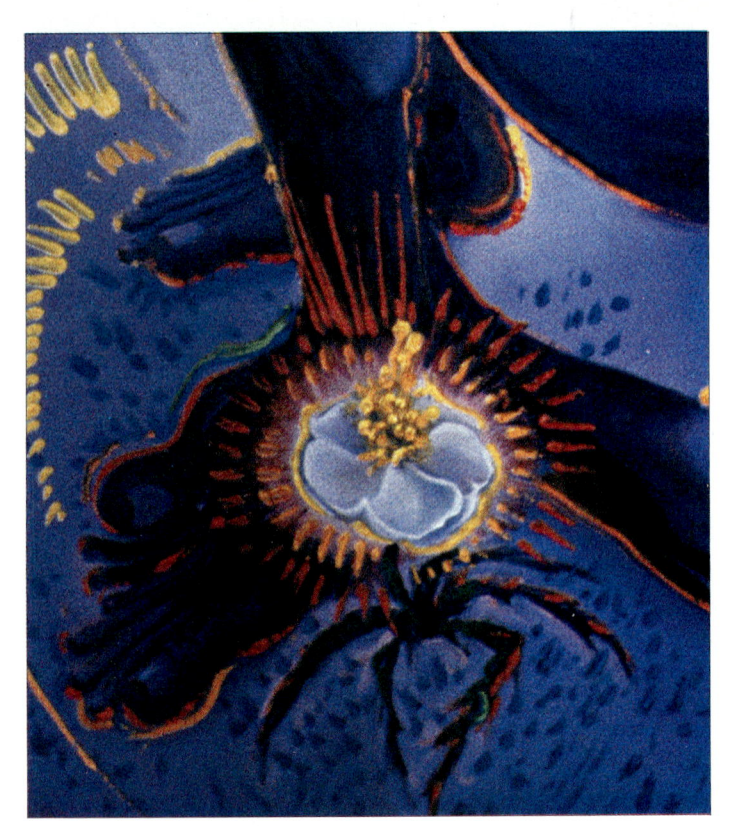

Garrett left her native Ireland as a young woman and lived in London and the south of France before settling down in New York, becoming an American citizen, and undertaking a successful career in publishing. This was a reasonable enough direction for her life to take. From her youth, she had been something of a pet among the British literati, and her friends and acquaintances included D. H. Lawrence, William Butler Yeats, George Bernard Shaw, Thomas Mann, Aldous Huxley, Robert Graves, and H. G. Wells.

A pensive youth (above) and a dramatic flower appear to be surrounded by auras in these oil paintings by the widely tested psychic Ingo Swann.

In 1951, Garrett founded the Parapsychology Foundation, which supported scholarly and scientific research. The venture was funded mostly by the wealthy Ohio philanthropist Frances T. Bolton, who admired Garrett and was fascinated by paranormal phenomena. Over the years, other adherents of the medium also contributed, and Garrett volunteered money of her own. Through the organization, she funded expeditions to many parts of the world, spreading her passion to define and explain psychic powers. According to some of her friends, she was generous to a fault. Psychic researcher and anthropologist Eric J. Dingwall, who knew Garrett for almost half a century, sometimes despaired of her propensity for handing out money to almost any alleged researcher who asked for it. "It was but rarely that I succeeded in persuading her to refuse a grant to some patent swindler," Dingwall said. " 'You never know,' she used to say, 'there might be something and we mustn't miss it, must we?' "

Garrett's fascination with the mysterious and arcane seemed inbred and inexhaustible. She took an interest in voodoo, which she studied in Haiti and Jamaica. As a young woman Garrett even investigated the practice of devil worship, though more in a spirit of curiosity than commitment. She also submitted herself to the scrutiny of psychiatrists, psychologists, and neurologists, as well as to J. B. Rhine and other serious parapsychologists.

One famous experiment in 1931 tested Garrett's supposed ability to leave her body while in a trance and report on distant scenes she saw in her astral state. In a New York apartment, a psychiatrist and a secretary looked on while the medium tried to see into a doctor's office in Reykjavik, Iceland. In preparation for the experiment, the doctor had placed a number of items on an office table. Garrett was supposed to describe them. While in a trance, she did so, and then went on to repeat verbatim a passage from a book the physician was reading while the test took place. In addition, she reported that the doctor's head was bandaged. The doctor confirmed later that she had identified the objects correctly, quoted the book accurately, and, because of a slight accident that happened just before the experiment, his head had indeed been bandaged. He also reported sensing Garrett's presence in his office during the test.

Along with participating in experiments, Garrett tried to advance research by traveling widely to lecture on psychic phenomena—to Switzerland, Spain, the Scandinavian countries, Austria, Germany, Italy, Greece, India, Japan, and parts of South America. In the course of her travels, she would, if asked, conduct séances. But these meetings were not public events. Rather, they consisted of only small groups, often of only one or two friends.

As a medium, Garrett purportedly worked with several spirit guides, or controls, who identified themselves as long-dead individuals. Chief among the controls was an Oriental personage called Uvani. Seeming to act as a sort of doorkeeper, Uvani controlled access for the other spirits seeking to speak through Garrett.

A hallmark of Garrett's fifty-year career as a medium was a reputation for honesty. She never took money for her séances. And, though she worked in a time when spiritualism was under attack and many mediums were exposed as frauds, she remained beyond reproach. This is not to say, however, that her accuracy was beyond question. In fact, the results of one of her most famous mediumistic triumphs were subject to considerable debate.

The séance took place in London on October 7, 1930. It was organized by Harry Price, director of the National Laboratory of Psychic Research, who was one of three people seated at the séance table. By his side his secretary, a Miss Ethel Beenham, edged forward on her chair, her notebook poised, while an Australian newspaperman named Ian Coster nervously twined and unlaced his fingers. The evening had begun with talk about the most sensational current news. Two days before, the British dirigible R-101, the largest and costliest airship built to date, had crashed in northern France during its maiden voyage. In the ensuing explosions and fire, all but six of the fifty-four people on board perished. Among the dead was Flight Lieutenant Carmichael Irwin, the dirigible's commander. Newspapers bulged with accounts of the disaster, the worst in British aviation history at the time, and controversy raged over whether England's ambitious airship program should be jettisoned altogether.

The three séance participants had discussed the subject at some length, but now they were silent, all staring expectantly at the stylish woman slumped in an armchair. If her companions were almost feverishly anticipatory, she seemed unaware of it—or perhaps even bored by it. She was, as Coster later wrote, "yawning her head off."

The séance followed by three months the death of Sir Arthur Conan Doyle, the creator of Sherlock Holmes. A devout spiritualist, Conan Doyle was convinced that the living could commune with those who had crossed to the other side, as his fellow believers were wont to say. Thus it did not seem unreasonable to expect that he himself might be accessible postmortem. So thinking, and sensing a possible sensational story, journalist Coster had asked Price to find the most reliable and respected medium in England to summon Conan Doyle's spirit. Price chose Eileen Garrett, the lady in the armchair.

Settling deeper into her cushion, Garrett breathed heavily and evenly, seeming to drift toward deep sleep. But no sooner had she closed her blue-green eyes than they began to gush tears, to the onlookers' astonishment. Uvani made only a brief appearance before an urgent voice interrupted him. "The whole bulk of the dirigible was . . . too much for her engine capacity," the male voice stuttered. The startled observers could see the psychic speaking, but the voice coming from her mouth certainly was not Garrett's, nor was it Uvani's, nor was it the restrained delivery of Conan Doyle. The speaker was agitated, panicky. "Useful lift too small," he said. "Gross lift computed badly . . . elevator jammed. Oil pipe plugged." On and on he went. Miss Beenham scribbled shorthand notes, her eyes glassy with amazement. Along with the others, she had read with horrified fascination the newspaper accounts of the R-101 disaster. No one had any trouble recognizing the man who was speaking through the medium. It seemed that Flight Lieutenant Irwin was describing in great technical detail the crash that had killed him two days before.

Sometime after Irwin finished his account, Conan Doyle did impart a message through Mrs. Garrett. At that point, however, the séance attendees regarded his contribution as a distinct anticlimax.

Garrett knew nothing about the mechanics of dirigibles, yet somehow she—or whoever was speaking through her—had spouted all sorts of technical aerodynamic details. Price rushed a transcript of the performance to the R-101's builders at the Royal Airship Works in Cardington. It was directed to a

A rare photograph from the 1930s shows Eileen Garrett, seated on a day bed, going into a trance while two other séance participants await revelations. Describing her trances, the medium said that "the space behind the forehead clears and becomes suffused with soft light in which changing colors play an important part, and I actually enter a dimension which is color."

man named Charlton, described by Price as an "acclaimed expert" on the majestic zeppelin. The alleged expert declared himself astounded by the accuracy of Garrett's technical descriptions and her revelations of secret details about the airship. In fact, however, Charlton was not an engineer or an aviator, but one of 400 members of the Cardington ground crew. His expertise was thus much in question, as was his objectivity: He was, as it turned out, a spiritualist. When the same document Charlton had reviewed was shown to two high-ranking, well-qualified members of the airship team, they adjudged that most of the vaunted technical details that Garrett had spouted were dead wrong.

In addition, Charlton's contention that secret details came out at the séance was hard to credit, since virtually nothing about the R-101 was secret. The dirigible was a pet project of Britain's Labour party, then in power. The government, competing with a private company that was building a similar craft, was anxious to get the ship airborne to prove the superiority of state ownership over private enterprise. Thus bureaucrats were constantly dismissing objections from scientists that numerous technical problems had to be resolved before the zeppelin could safely fly. The whole matter became a subject of great public debate, and most anyone who cared to follow it in the newspapers knew almost all there was to know about the ill-fated R-101.

Nevertheless, Garrett's R-101 séance gained instant fame and easily outstripped the facts on its way to becoming legend. At the time, not even skeptics cared to call the lady a liar; her reputation was far too pristine. Rather, it was suggested that the medium had somehow picked up telepathic emanations from Coster, who, being a journalist, probably would have been familiar with at least some specifics about the dirigible and its problems. As was her habit, Garrett herself offered no assessment of the matter and left the debate about the séance to others.

Although her purported psychic gifts centered on mediumship, Garrett commonly experienced more straightforward psychic episodes as well. She was dining with friends at the Savoy Hotel in London one night during World War I when

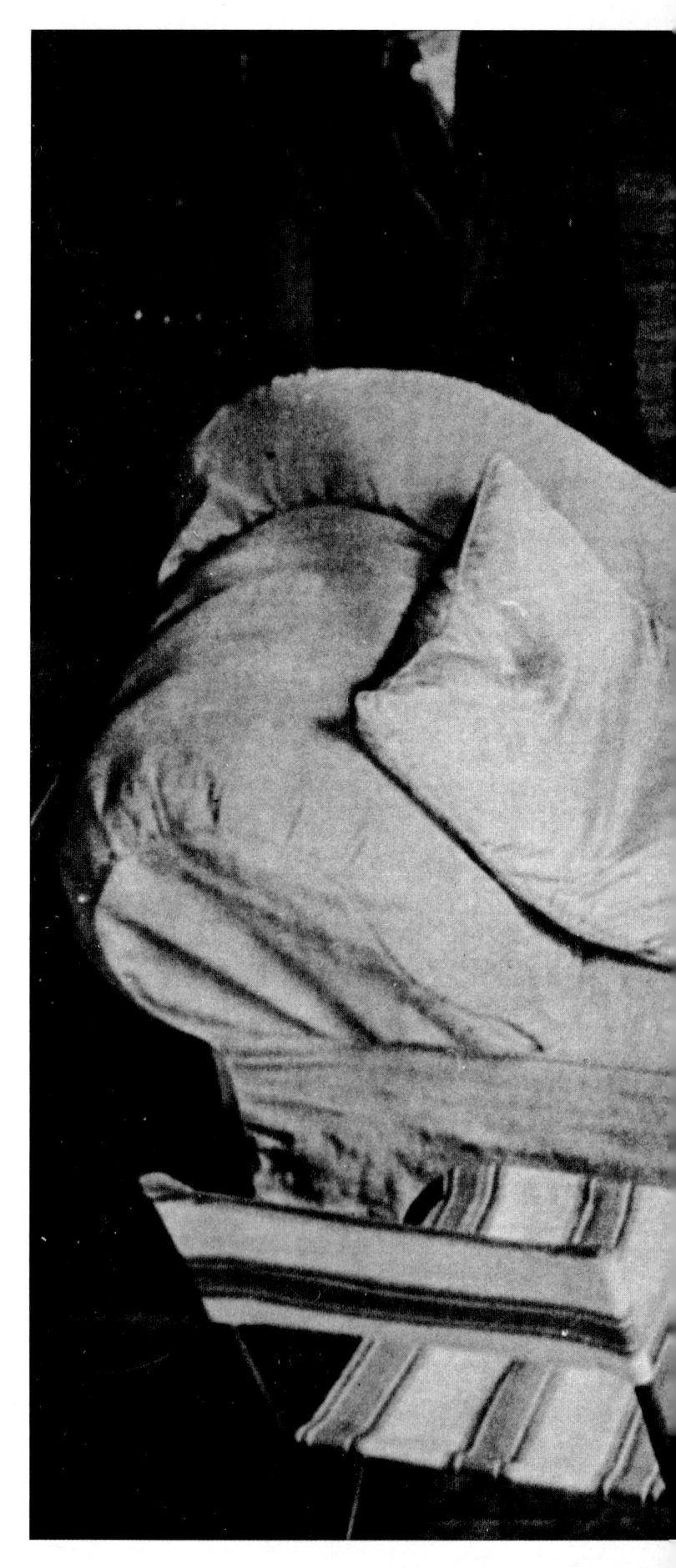

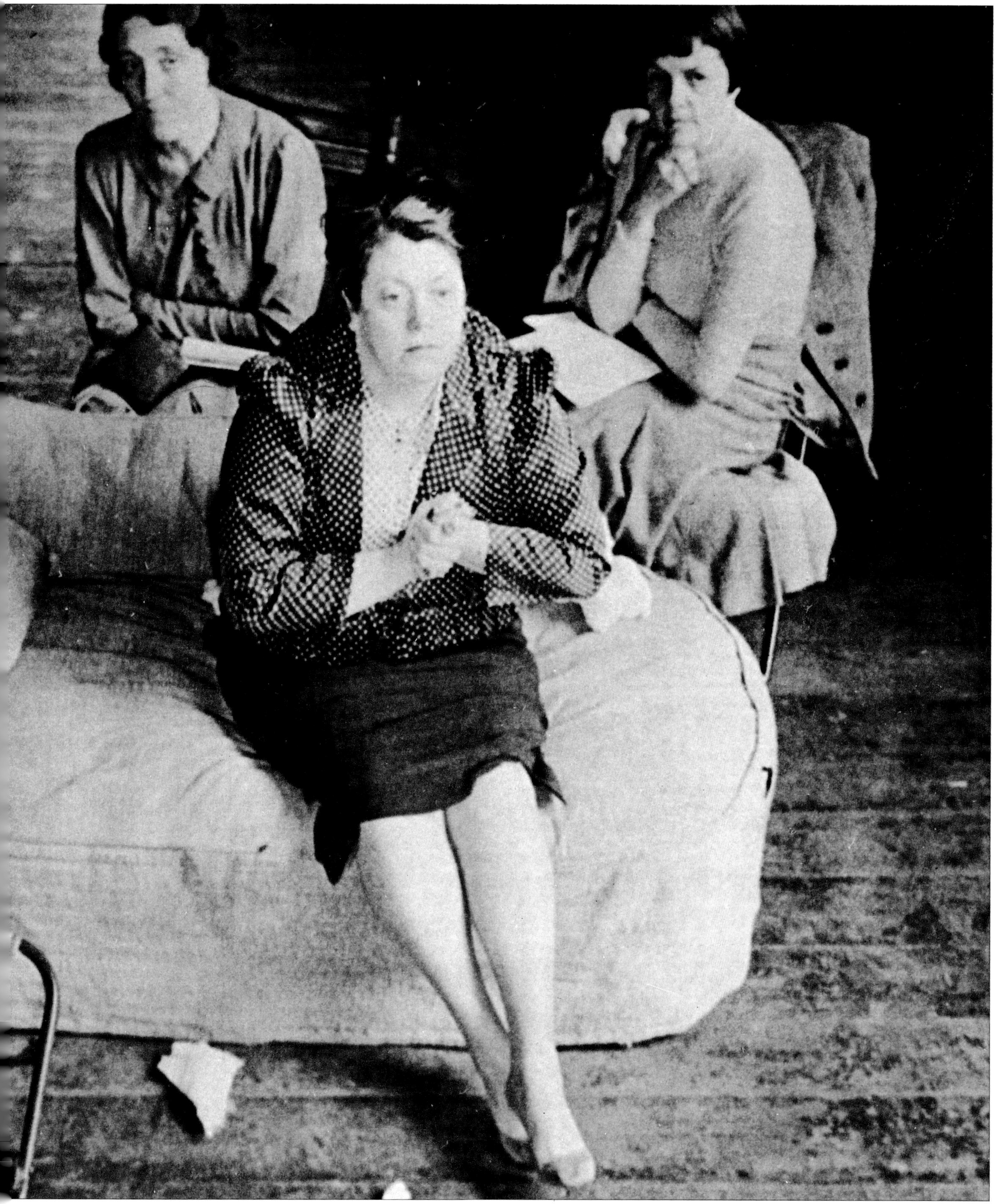

she suddenly felt herself surrounded by reeking fumes and the sounds of war. At the same time, she had a horrifying clairvoyant vision of her young husband and several other men being blown up on a battlefield. A few days later, the British War Office advised her that her husband was among the missing. He had gone on a wire-cutting mission and not returned, and the War Office was never able to supply details of his death. "Only I knew the manner in which he had died," the psychic wrote at a later date.

Eileen Coley has said that her mother considered her unusual talents more a burden than a blessing, and her long search to explain them was a way of exorcising the affliction and trying to turn it to good use. "Why should she be stuck with this business, she felt, unless she could find out some way it could be used for the good of other human beings?" the daughter said. Garrett encouraged the laboratory approach to unraveling the mystery, as she encouraged all inquiry. But she observed that "any attempt to explain the psyche and its manifold patterns in terms of language gets bogged down. The answer may well come from other aspects of science as yet not heard from officially." Finally, her quest was as inconclusive as it was thorough. It was not the habit of most mediums to doubt the utter veracity of their spirit guides, but Garrett, a lifelong skeptic despite her seeming gifts, was always dubious about the true nature of hers. In her autobiography, she theorized that the controls might have been no more than manifestations from her own subconscious. Beyond that, she knew of them only what she was told, she said, since she had never met them. Necessarily, they were present only when she was unconscious.

As to her purported powers of clairvoyance, telepathy, and precognition, Garrett was certain only that there was nothing supernatural, or even paranormal, about them. She speculated that they might have originated in the hypothalamus gland, or in the vestigial animal brain at the base of the skull. Animals seemed able to sense danger in ways unrelated to the five senses, she posited, while in most hu-

Perhaps the only photograph ever taken of an Edgar Cayce reading was published by the Chicago Examiner on February 19, 1911. In it, the so-called sleeping prophet reclines on a couch while his father, Leslie B. Cayce, conducts the reading and a stenographer takes notes. Edgar Cayce did more than 14,000 such readings in his lifetime; most dealt with psychic healing.

mans that knack might have atrophied beneath the weight of prodigious forebrains.

Secure in her powers but still unsure of their origins, Garrett died in France September 15, 1970, at the age of 77. Nearly two decades after her death, her Parapsychology Foundation still continued her work under Eileen Coley's stewardship. Coley's own daughter worked there as well, making three generations of Garrett women who had furthered efforts to chart the world of psychic powers.

Although Garrett and Edgar Cayce were contemporaries and had in common the apparent ability to transcend their own psyches, they could scarcely have been more different. Garrett was a brilliant, sophisticated, much-traveled, and worldly woman. Cayce was an unlettered rustic from rural Kentucky. Garrett spent a lifetime seeking to explore and develop her talents. Cayce was a somewhat reluctant seer, troubled through much of his life by his strange gifts. Cayce and Garrett met once, in the 1930s, and did readings for each other. Although associates of both said the psychics had great respect for each other, the single meeting did not produce a close friendship. Whatever the two may have had in common in matters of spirit, they were worlds apart in matters of style.

According to his biographers, Cayce's psychic turning point came on a fine May afternoon in 1890 when he was thirteen years old. He was sitting in the woods on the family farm near Hopkinsville, Kentucky, enjoying a favorite pastime—reading the Bible. Suddenly, he realized he was not alone. He looked up to see a woman standing before him. At first he thought it was his mother: The sun was bright behind her, and it was difficult to see. But when she spoke, he realized she was not anyone that he knew. Her voice was uncommonly soft and musical.

"Your prayers have been heard," she said. "Tell me what you would like most of all, so that I may give it to you."

Though frightened, the teenager stammered an answer: "Most of all I would like to be helpful to others, especially to children when they are sick."

Without reply the woman vanished into the sunbeams.

Edgar's first reaction was to fear he might be going crazy. But following on the heels of the vision was an indication that, indeed, he had been given some special power.

Edgar had never done well in school. His teachers complained that he was dreamy and inattentive. These failings much displeased his father, a no-nonsense fellow called Squire Cayce by his neighbors because he was the local justice of the peace. The night after the vision, Edgar was studying his spelling primer—as usual, without much luck—when the elder Cayce decided to take matters in hand. Father and son sat at a table with the book between them. Over the course of a long evening, the father intoned one word after another, and the son spelled most of them incorrectly. At half past ten, the boy heard the lady in the woods saying, "If you can sleep a little, we can help you." Begging the squire for a short respite, Edgar curled up in a chair with the spelling book under his head and fell asleep instantly.

When the lesson resumed a few minutes after he woke, the story goes, Edgar's answers were rapid and correct. To his father's astonishment, he went on to spell words from future lessons and even to specify which words were on which page and what illustrations went with them. For the rest of his life, Edgar Cayce allegedly maintained this clairvoyant ability to absorb near-photographic images of printed matter when, literally, he slept on it.

Not long after the spelling incident, young Edgar had an accident. In games during recess at school, a pitched ball hit him near the base of the spine. There was no apparent serious injury, but for the rest of the day he behaved oddly. At dinner that night, the normally reserved boy threw things at his three

All big cities have their share of professed psychic advisers. Those pictured here and on the next seven pages work in or near London, England. Steve Speed, shown above, is a psychometrist. Holding an object, he purports to read in its psychic vibrations clues about its owner.

sisters and taunted his father. Stranger yet, when he went to bed and fell asleep, he began to talk. He told his parents he was in shock. To cure it, he said, they should make a poultice of cornmeal, onions, and herbs, and apply it to the back of his head. They did. The next morning he remembered nothing at all of the day before, but he was back to normal. It seemed that he had just delivered his first psychic reading.

During the eleven years following these two curious episodes, Cayce made scant use of his apparent psychic power. He was ill at ease with it. A deeply religious fundamentalist Christian, he was unsure whether his gift came from God or the devil or why, in either case, it should have devolved on him. It is possible he might have continued trying to ignore his talents indefinitely had he not, in 1900, lost his voice.

It was a peculiar infirmity in that doctors found no apparent physical cause for it, yet it persisted into 1901. This came at a particularly troublesome time. Cayce was just starting to make his way as an apprentice photographer, hoping to earn enough money to marry his fiancée, Gertrude Evans. Being unable to talk above a muffled rasp was interfering with both his career and his courtship. Near despair, Cayce turned for a cure to hypnotism, which was much in vogue in the United States at the time.

A local hypnotist named Al C. Layne, familiar with the squire's tale of Edgar's poultice cure, proposed putting the younger Cayce into a trance and having him diagnose himself. Edgar agreed to try. On a Sunday afternoon in March, Layne was ushered into the parlor of the Cayce farmhouse, where the squire and Edgar waited. Layne began talking softly, trying to induce a trance, but his patient interrupted. There was no need for such an effort, Edgar said. He often put himself "to sleep." It was no trouble at all. Layne should just concentrate on making the proper suggestions once Edgar was under. With that, the young man sighed deeply and slipped instantly into what appeared to be profound slumber. Layne then suggested that Edgar look inside his own body and pinpoint the trouble with his throat.

As his biographers would have it later, the entranced Cayce began to mumble at first, and then the young man began to speak in a clear voice. "Yes," he said, "we can see the body. In the normal state this body is unable to speak due to a partial paralysis of the inferior muscles of the vocal cords, produced by nerve strain. This is a psychological condition producing a physical effect. This may be removed by increasing the circulation to the affected parts by suggestion while in this unconscious condition."

The squire and the hypnotist were amazed. Edgar did not ordinarily talk that way. Awake, he might not have been able to pronounce some of those words, let alone understand them. Nevertheless, Layne gave the instructed suggestion. He and the squire looked on for the next twenty minutes while the skin over Edgar's throat and upper chest turned pink, then rose, then crimson with heightened blood flow. Finally, the sleeping man spoke.

"It is all right now," he said. "The condition is removed. Make the suggestion that the circulation return to normal, and that after that the body awaken." When Cayce awoke, his voice was fully restored.

Layne, who dabbled in osteopathy, argued that Cayce should use his apparent gift for psychic healing to help others. At first, Cayce resisted. He knew nothing about his unconscious pronouncements except what he was told, and certainly he had no conscious control over them. He feared he might harm the very people he was trying to help. But finally, reluctantly, he agreed it was his duty to try.

Over the next twenty-two years, Cayce did thousands of medical readings. Twice a day he would lie down and "sleep," as he regarded it. In this altered state, which resembled a self-induced hypnotic trance, he would answer requests for psychic healing. As newspapers began spreading reports of his work, those requests began coming in from throughout the United States. Cayce dealt with as many of these requests as time permitted. Apparently, distance was no barrier to his alleged mental probes, since he often did readings for clients who were hundreds of miles away. In time he came to have thousands of enthusiastic supporters. But, of course, there were detractors as well.

A very private man, Cayce suffered under the notoriety his work occasioned, and he was mortified by the inevitable accusations of fraud. In November of 1931, during a brief visit to meet with admirers in New York, he ran afoul of the law. He had acceded to two women's request for a reading, but the women turned out to be police officers and Cayce was arrested. He was charged under a 1927 New York statute making it a misdemeanor to tell fortunes for money or with intent to defraud. At a hearing before a magistrate, Cayce was asked about claims that he was a psychic. "I make no claims whatever," he answered. "For thirty-one years I have been told I was a psychic. It first began as a child. I didn't know what it was. After it had gone on for years, a company was formed to study my work."

The company in question was the Association for Research and Enlightenment (ARE), founded by Cayce adherents earlier in 1931 to study and preserve his work. The magistrate, deciding that the ARE was an "incorporated ecclesiastical body," threw the case out of court. The police had no right, the magistrate stated, to tamper with the beliefs of an ecclesiastical body. Besides, he did not believe Cayce intended any fraud.

Despite the favorable outcome, the case was enough to exacerbate the psychic's considerable self-doubt and send him into a depression. As he had several times during his career, he wondered if his apparent psychic gifts were either valid or useful, and he considered giving up the work.

Cayce sometimes longed for the kind of widespread legitimacy that seemed to elude him for much of his lifetime, but he was unsure how to pursue it. Submitting himself to testing by parapsychologists had little appeal, since he had acquired an early and deep distrust of scientific inquiry.

In 1906, when he was living in Bowling Green, Kentucky, Cayce let a physician friend persuade him to give a reading before an audience that included other doctors. Once Cayce was unconscious, a debate arose in the audience about the exact nature of his condition. Some argued for self-hypnosis, others for trance or dream, still others for simple fakery. One doctor stuck a needle in Cayce's arms, hands, and feet to see how the psychic would react. When there was no response to that assault, another physician pushed a hatpin all the way through the sleeping man's cheek.

"He's hardened to all of that," said a third skeptic, who then took out a penknife and partially excised the nail from Cayce's left forefinger. There was still no indication of pain and no blood, but when Cayce awoke he was in agony. In a rare loss of temper he berated his tormentors and, before walking out, declared: "I'll never try to prove anything to any one of you again."

Cayce was at odds with most traditional physicians, largely because of his medical unorthodoxy. His adherents have assessed his diagnostic accuracy at eighty-five percent. However, that figure was arrived at in a random sampling of only about .5 percent of the available data. The therapies he prescribed were eclectic and hard to classify. They encompassed osteopathy, chemotherapy, hydrotherapy, nutrition, chiropractic, massage, and home remedies. Some of the therapies were decidedly bizarre. For example, when his wife, Gertrude, was diagnosed as having terminal tuberculosis, he ordered a regimen entailing a special diet, small doses of heroin, the application of a poultice made of crushed grapes, and sniffing apple brandy fumes from a charred wooden keg. She made a complete recovery.

However, not all of Cayce's psychic healing went so well, and some cases were demonstrable failures. For instance, he once gave a long diagnosis for a little girl suffering from leukemia and recommended a complicated dietary treatment. Unfortunately, the child had died the day before the reading was given—a fact Cayce somehow failed to divine. In another case, he advised the following recipe for an ailing male patient: Boil together wild cherry bark, sarsaparilla root, wild ginger, Indian turnip, wild ginseng, prickly ash bark, buchu, and mandrake root. Add grain alcohol and tolu balsam. Administer for ten days.

The efficacy of this odd nostrum was not to be tested. Again, as it turned out, the psychic was prescribing for a patient who had already died.

Still, many of Cayce's clientele did report remarkable cures and were more than happy to pay for them. Nevertheless, Cayce intensely disliked taking money in return for his services. Although he was often on the edge of penury himself, he began accepting fees regularly only when, in middle age,

Armed with birth dates and times, high-tech psychic Bettina Lee uses a computer to cast astrology charts for her clients. She uses her supposed psychic powers to interpret the charts.

he concluded that he was fated for his psychic work. Not until 1923 did he give up photography and all other attempts at business and begin devoting full time to the readings. Even then, he never refused petitioners because they lacked the wherewithal to pay for his services.

Cayce's career took on a new dimension that same year. The instigator of the change was Arthur Lammers, who was a wealthy printer from Dayton, Ohio. Lammers sought out Cayce for some readings, but he did not want answers to health problems. Rather, he asked about such things as esoteric astrology, the workings of the subconscious, and the nature of spirit and soul. He mentioned the mystery religions of Egypt and Greece and Tibet and the Jewish cabala, along with alchemy, yoga, and theosophy.

Cayce had only the faintest idea of what the man was talking about, and he was not at all sure he wanted to know more. Once again, he felt a threat to his fundamentalist Christianity. What if Lammers was leading him to sacrilege? Eventually, however, Cayce let himself be persuaded to work with Lammers. Lammers argued that the ideas of one God, of the need for human morality and brotherhood, were common to all the great metaphysical systems. If Cayce could clear up the confusion that reigned beyond those central tenets, then it was his duty to do it.

Cayce gave a reading for Lammers that began with astrology. Its end result, however, was to confirm the reality of reincarnation. Humans did, indeed, experience successive lifetimes for the purpose of perfecting their souls, the ultimate aim being the union of those souls with God.

In time, Cayce's consternation at his own pronouncement gave way to belief. Once he was able to reconcile the idea of reincarnation with his Christian faith, he enthusiastically added metaphysical readings to his purely physical ones. He developed what he called a life reading. Starting with astrological conditions of the subject's birth, the life reading would then turn to several of the individual's alleged past incarnations. The aim of a life reading was to find information from past lives that would make one's present existence happier and more fruitful.

When he was unconscious, Cayce always spoke of himself in the third person, which augmented the impression of some strange bifurcation in his personality. Awake, the mild-mannered provincial had no explanation for his seeming magic. However, once, in his altered state, he gave this assessment of his psychic powers:

"Edgar Cayce's mind is amenable to suggestion, the same as all other subconscious minds, but in addition thereto it has the power to interpret to the objective mind of others what it acquires from the subconscious mind of other individuals of the same kind. The subconscious mind forgets nothing. The conscious mind receives the impression from without and transfers all thought to the subconscious, where it remains even though the conscious be destroyed."

Some analysts of Cayce's work have categorized his power as clairvoyance—an ability to see into bodies at a distance to diagnose ailments, as well as a talent for peering into the past and future. However, Cayce and his family saw it more as telepathy—mind-to-mind communication—but on a subconscious level. In addition, Cayce seemed to be saying that he could telepathically tap into the knowledge of some transcendental mind, perhaps akin to what psychologist Carl Jung called the collective unconscious.

Cayce himself described this cosmic mind pool as God's book of remembrance or the universal consciousness. He also used a term that would eventually be popularized by New Age psychics who came after him—the akashic records. The term was derived from the Hindu theosophical word *akasa,* referring to a primary creative principle of nature. The authoritative *Encyclopedia of Occultism and Parapsychology* gives the definition of the akashic records as "a kind of central filing system of all events, thoughts and actions impressed upon an astral plane, which may be consulted in certain conditions of consciousness." Events so recorded on the astral ether were thought to be "reanimated by mystics like a celestial television set."

It was Cayce's habit to have someone take notes during his readings. In the early years, the transcriptionist would be his father or his wife, but in 1923, he hired Gladys Davis as a full-time secretary. Thereafter, there was a verbatim record of all his work. When Edgar Cayce died in 1945, he left behind more than 14,000 recorded readings, the great majority dealing either with physical ailments or with past lives of his clients. All remain on file in Virginia Beach, Virginia, at the headquarters of the ARE, which continues to flourish under the aegis of his two sons.

The ARE today claims a membership of more than 30,000 people. Thousands more belong to many "Search for God" study groups that pursue Cayce's work. These are located on every continent in the world except Antarctica. Some one hundred books have been written about the sleeping prophet, and collectively they have sold more than twelve million copies. No psychic, not even Eileen Garrett, has ever approached Edgar Cayce in popular appeal.

That appeal cannot be explained fully in terms of the knowledge he claimed to tap, phenomenal though it was. Rather, his enduring influence seems more a product of the man himself, the waking Cayce—gentle, unassuming, much-beleaguered, and perfectly ordinary. If Mrs. Garrett was the grand doyenne of the psychic world, Cayce was its quintessential common man. He was, as his chief biographer, Thomas Sugrue, once commented, "just an American guy." Precisely because of his ordinariness, hundreds of thousands of people who were not rich or famous or well connected could identify with him. They believed that if a man like Cayce could somehow enter a mysterious world that was finer, loftier, and

John Lindsay's technique combines palmistry, numerology, and tarot. He begins a sitting by checking the client's hands for suppleness, size, and the length and shape of fingers.

saner than this one, and if a powerless man could call on great power, then maybe anybody could. Certainly, in his wake, many have tried.

By the mid-1980s, believers in psychic phenomena had become a majority in America; two-thirds of American adults reported to pollsters that they had experienced psychic events. Among these millions, some belong to that multifocused kaleidoscope of disparate beliefs and pursuits that is the New Age subculture.

New Agers have no central organization, hierarchy, or common dogma. Their interests are extraordinarily diverse. Some are mild adherents who practice holistic health or try honing their psi potential as a hobby. Others are dedicated practitioners who build lifestyles around ancient mystery religions or the pronouncements of disembodied spirits.

Although most New Agers share an interest in psychic powers, there is some disagreement within the movement over what the word *psychic* means. Does it stop with mind reading, remote viewing, and seeing the past and future? Or does it apply in some general sense to all things that are arcane, occult, or spiritual? Cayce looked to the word's Greek origin, *psyche,* or soul, and defined it as "spirit, soul, or the imagination of the mind," having to do with things "not understood from the physical, or material, or conscious mind." For the most part, it is in this cosmic sense that things psychic underpin the New Age.

What all New Agers share is a search for some metaphysical meaning in life. In addition, most believe in the possibility of transcending the mundane world in one way or another, whether by meditating on crystals or by studying with gurus or by any number of other vehicles.

Although detractors tend to regard them as holdover hippies or dwellers on the social fringe, New Agers hardly fit that profile. Neither are they a credulous, ignorant undercaste. SRI International estimated in 1987 that movement members made up some five to ten percent of the American population and that most were in their thirties or forties, affluent, and well educated. Especially in the cities, having a personal psychic adviser had become as chic for young professionals as driving the proper car or maintaining an exclusive address.

Thousands of enthusiasts have joined self-help groups, which operate toward the conservative end of the New Age spectrum and are akin to the so-called human potential movements popular in the 1970s. For instance, the Spiritual Frontiers Fellowship in New York sponsors lectures, seminars, and workshops on developing spirituality. The Fellowship, which utilizes the teachings of Cayce, among others, believes that psychic powers are often a by-product of the spiritual quest. Headquartered in Sedona, Arizona, a nonprofit organization called Free Soul seeks to explore the human spirit by means of biofeedback, meditation, and mind and body control. One aim is to cultivate psychic sensitivity for use in daily living. Free Soul has upward of two hundred instructors working throughout the United States and a clientele of approximately 25,000 people. Each pays ten dollars per lesson for the Free Soul instruction.

Some organizations offer almost limitless options for psi buffs. In New York City the Open Center, the Circle of Light Institute, and the Learning Annex provide past-life regressions, aura reading, and even telepathic communion with the psychic energy of whales. Venice, California, is headquarters for the Conscious Connection, once a metaphysical meeting ground for single men and women but now open to all. It features the full psychic menu, but for the truly venturesome—skeptics might say the truly credulous—the Connection touts its centerpiece subgroup, the Channeling Network.

Channelers—the term has supplanted *mediums*—are a New Age passion. They purport to be pipelines for disembodied spirits, whether of long-dead humans or entities who never lived on this earthly plane. The Channeling Network offers a selection of channelers to accommodate the needs of a varied, but generally well-to-do, clientele. One of this number is Shawn Randall, who hosts a spirit adviser called Torah. Torah is described as an "interdimensional consciousness," and, according to Randall, is "a pretty easy guy to talk with." Torah regresses Randall's clients through past lives and, like most good spirits affiliated with channelers, gives advice on temporal problems. Some channelers specialize in dead celebrities. California-based William Tenuto claims to produce the late Beatle John Lennon, not to mention Jesus Christ. Tenuto says he has channeled Jesus often enough to call him "a good friend."

Channeling is a growth industry, complete with agents. New York's Cosmic Contact Psychic Services, the first agency to represent so-called paranormal professionals, includes channelers along with its more traditional astrologers, palmists, and tarot readers. Perhaps the most successful channeling entrepreneur, however, is a strictly freelance one-time homemaker from Yelm, Washington, named J. Z. Knight. Her claim to superterrestrial contact is as conduit for Ramtha, purportedly a 35,000-year-old warrior from the lost continent of Lemuria. Ramtha is quite a draw. In a husky voice that affects a variety of accents, he addresses large crowds in weekend seminars that cost $400 per person. The message is consistent with much New Age teaching: Everyone bears God within; there is no right or wrong, just individual reality; each person has the power to control his or her destiny. Knight's own destiny is getting along handsomely. Her income from Ramtha-related enterprises is said to run into the millions of dollars.

An estimated 2,500 New Age bookstores exist in America, and many New Age periodicals are available. Some specialize in networking information—about local witchcraft covens, for example. Some publications report heavily on personal mystical experiences. One popular magazine features interviews with dead celebrities.

The periodicals usually contain advertisements for all manner of occult talismans and psychic services. They tout books offering to reveal the ritual secrets of "Hopi sacred sweats" or detail the afterlives of plane-crash victims or teach the laws governing psychic assassinations. Psychics advertise to tap the universal consciousness for answers to petitioners' questions—all by mail and at the rate of only two dollars per answer, sometimes less.

These mail-order psychics occupy the low end of a psychic adviser hierarchy that is part of the New Age. Today, several hundred thousand psychic advisers are operating in the United States alone. Joining the mail-order contingent near the bottom of the scale are the old-style fortune tellers who use tea leaves or crystal balls, many of whom operate from shabby store fronts in the cities or from house trailers in the countryside. But there is also a new aristocracy of psychic advisers who are a far cry from the turbaned swamis or bejeweled gypsies of popular folklore. The new seers dress tastefully, live well, and command large fees from large followings. Some attract celebrity clients, and some of them are celebrities in their own right. Whether these advisers read tarot cards or astrology charts, they usually come equipped with business cards and press kits.

One such representative of the psychic elite is Patricia McLaine of Arlington, Virginia, just across the Potomac River from the capital city of Washington. Around four or five times each weekday, McLaine will sit with one of her clients in the sunny study of her suburban home and lay out the tarot cards that help guide her readings. She is not, however, always in residence there. She travels often to serve people in Texas and California. There are still other clients as far away as Europe, Asia, and Australia, with whom she confers by telephone. In all, she estimates that she has as many as 3,000 clients, most of whom, she says, come in for "a yearly checkup or a twice-a-year checkup." Her patrons include a number of well-known individuals, among them actress Shirley MacLaine, whose best-selling books and popular television movie about her own metaphysical search prompted a boomlet within the New Age movement. Featured in several books and magazine articles about psychics, Patricia McLaine is also a popular television talk-show guest.

Utilizing astrology as well as tarot, she usually gives readings that last for a half hour or an hour. She charges $65 for the shorter reading, $125 for the longer. In addition, her more affluent clients might request a master reading, which lasts several hours. The master reading, for which McLaine prepares with meditation and fasting in order to achieve a properly receptive state of mind, covers a sitter's past lives and the numerous intricate relationships that may be affecting the present existence.

"I don't think I would have become a psychic if I hadn't started reading Edgar Cayce books in the 1960s," McLaine says. In those days, she was an aspiring young playwright working as a secretary at the Twentieth Century Fox movie studio in Los Angeles. Inspired by what she read of Cayce, she began visiting psychics. After two of them told her that she herself would eventually become a psychic reader, she began doing free readings for her friends at the studio. McLaine's career developed from there.

She classifies herself as partly psychic but "at least 50 percent intuitive." There is, she says, a big difference. "The intuitive is superior to the psychic," she explains. "The psychic is receiving a feeling or an impression, and the intuitive level of knowledge is direct knowledge." A psychic impression is like "looking at something through a foot of water. You may see it correctly, you may not . . . or maybe you get a general impression, but it may not be the absolute." With intuition, though, one "can't be wrong."

Whatever her vehicle of access may be, McLaine describes the source of her psychic knowledge as "the great storehouse of the collective unconscious. That's where it all comes from. That's where it is created. People are creating their lives at all moments of all days. The psychic person is simply able to tune in to that."

Despite her success, McLaine has misgivings about her vocation. A serious student of metaphysics for more than twenty years, she began in 1975 to teach courses on tarot, the cabala, and other metaphysical subjects. She prefers teaching these subjects to being what she calls "an esoteric psychologist" for her clients. People are inclined to vest too much power in their psychic advisers, she says, rather than work toward enlightenment on their own.

"A lot of people are not willing to meditate and put the effort into spiritual study that is involved in developing your higher connection," she says. "They want it to be real easy and simple—'show me the fastest way to heaven.' There's one

A black orb of Venetian crystal figures in John Christopher Travers's readings, along with the tarot cards and a magnifying glass he uses to read the fine lines in his clients' hands.

creative process, and we are godlets. A master of wisdom would not sit down and read your cards for you, or do your planets for you, or give you a reading. He would try to give you principles by which to live in order to enhance your life."

McLaine attributes the modern psychic and spiritual revival to the fact that the so-called Age of Aquarius, which dawned in the 1960s, is just picking up steam in the 1980s. She hails the Aquarian Age, a term that is synonymous with the New Age, as a time of great spiritual awakening and evolution. Nevertheless, she acknowledges that not all psychics are equally talented—nor are they equally honest. "A lot of people in my business," she says, "are downright strange."

Indeed, debunkers of psychics pinpoint several techniques used by the dishonest to bilk clients. Chief among these is the so-called cold reading in which the psychic is able to satisfy a client by tossing out generalities and then detecting responses *(page 80)*. Part of the cold reading is the "stock spiel," wherein the sitter is offered a set of bland pronouncements that could apply to almost anyone. In many cases, the sitter's reactions to the spiel, both verbal and in body language, cue the alert reader to home in on a few particulars—enough, often, to convince the sitter that he or she has experienced a true psychic event.

Most well-known psychics of recent years have provided some psychic counseling for individual clients, but not all have specialized in it. For example, Chicago's Irene Hughes, although she is an adviser for several celebrities, is probably better known as a seer in the realm of public events. Among the more notable of her claimed precognitions were the assassinations of John and Robert Kennedy and Martin Luther King, Jr., the 1967 outbreak of the Arab-Israeli Six Day War, and President Lyndon B. Johnson's decision not to seek a second term. A popular television personality and newspaper columnist, the platinum-haired psychic was born Irene Finger in rural Tennessee, one of eleven children in a poor farm family. As a child, her feelings about incipient events supposedly proved accurate enough to prompt her father to consult her about when to pick cotton or when to expect rain.

Harking back to psychic superstars of an earlier generation, Hughes shared with Edgar Cayce a sylvan vision in childhood and with Eileen Garrett an Oriental spirit guide. When she was four, Hughes was alone in the woods when she allegedly was visited by a shimmering lady. The luminous vision described and validated the child's ability to feel strange and wonderful things not sensed by others. Some years later, the adult Hughes was recovering from surgery when she received another visit from a discarnate entity. As she lay at home in her sickbed, an Oriental man materialized in front of her and identified himself as Kaygee.

As Hughes later reported the conversation that followed, Kaygee described himself as "your control, your teacher, and your friend." He predicted that she would eventually learn "many things unknown to others" and would have "the key to all life." During the course of their meeting, Hughes said, Kaygee guided her through her incarnation in a past life in Egypt. Kaygee was supposedly a wise Japanese Christian who died in 1961. A devout Christian herself, Hughes considers her psychic abilities to be God-given.

Hughes is among many psychics who believe psychic talent is present, at least potentially, in everyone. But New York's Alex Tanous thinks himself uniquely marked from birth with signs of special gifts. Tanous is of Lebanese extraction, and his father was a friend of the famed Lebanese poet Kahlil Gibran. By the psychic's account, Gibran predicted to the elder Tanous before Alex's birth that the boy would become "a man of exceptional gifts, of great abilities." In addition, Tanous says, he was born with some lines in his palm forming a hexagram and others depicting a mystic cross, and still others spelling the name "Alex" backward. He was also born with a

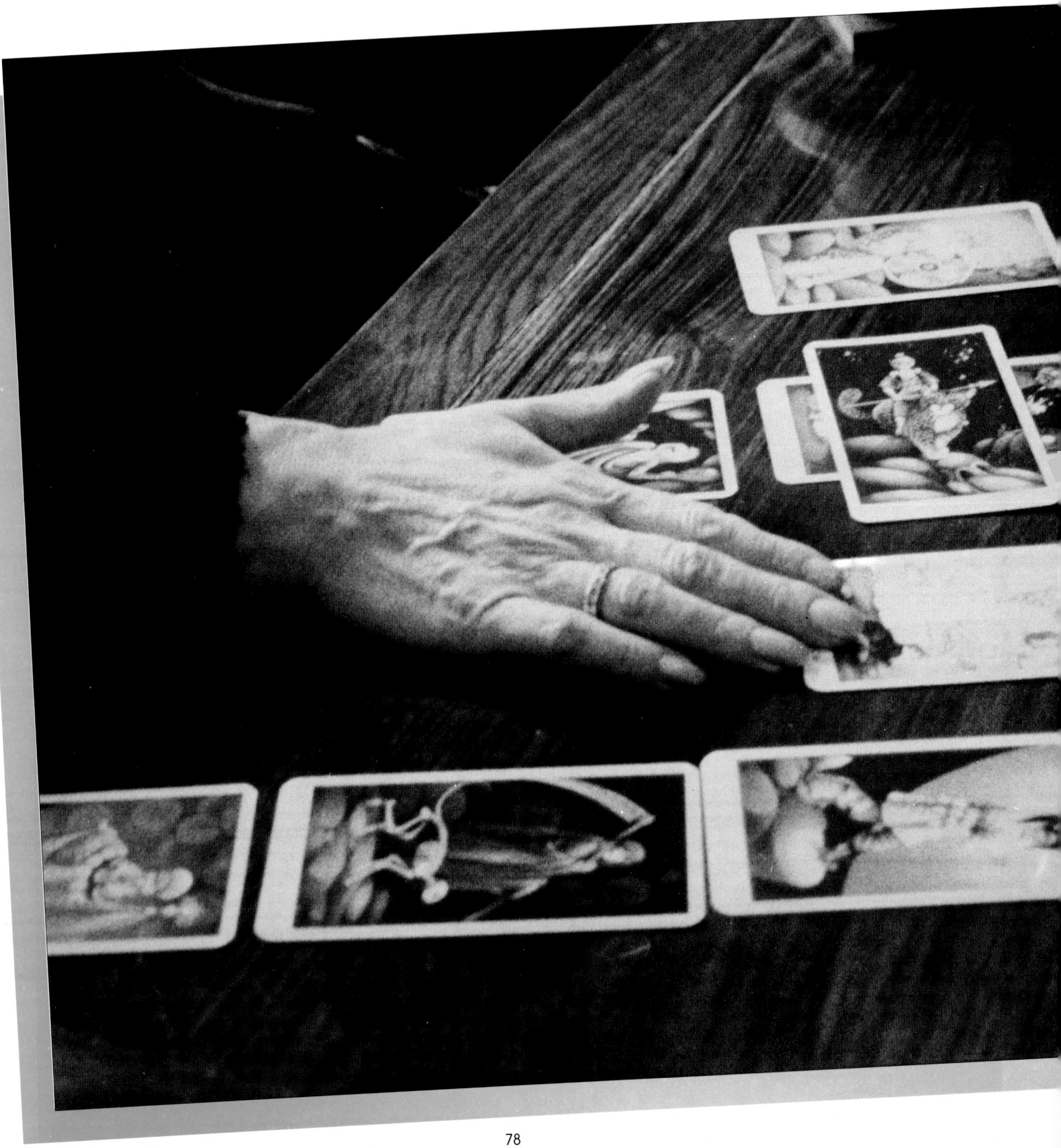

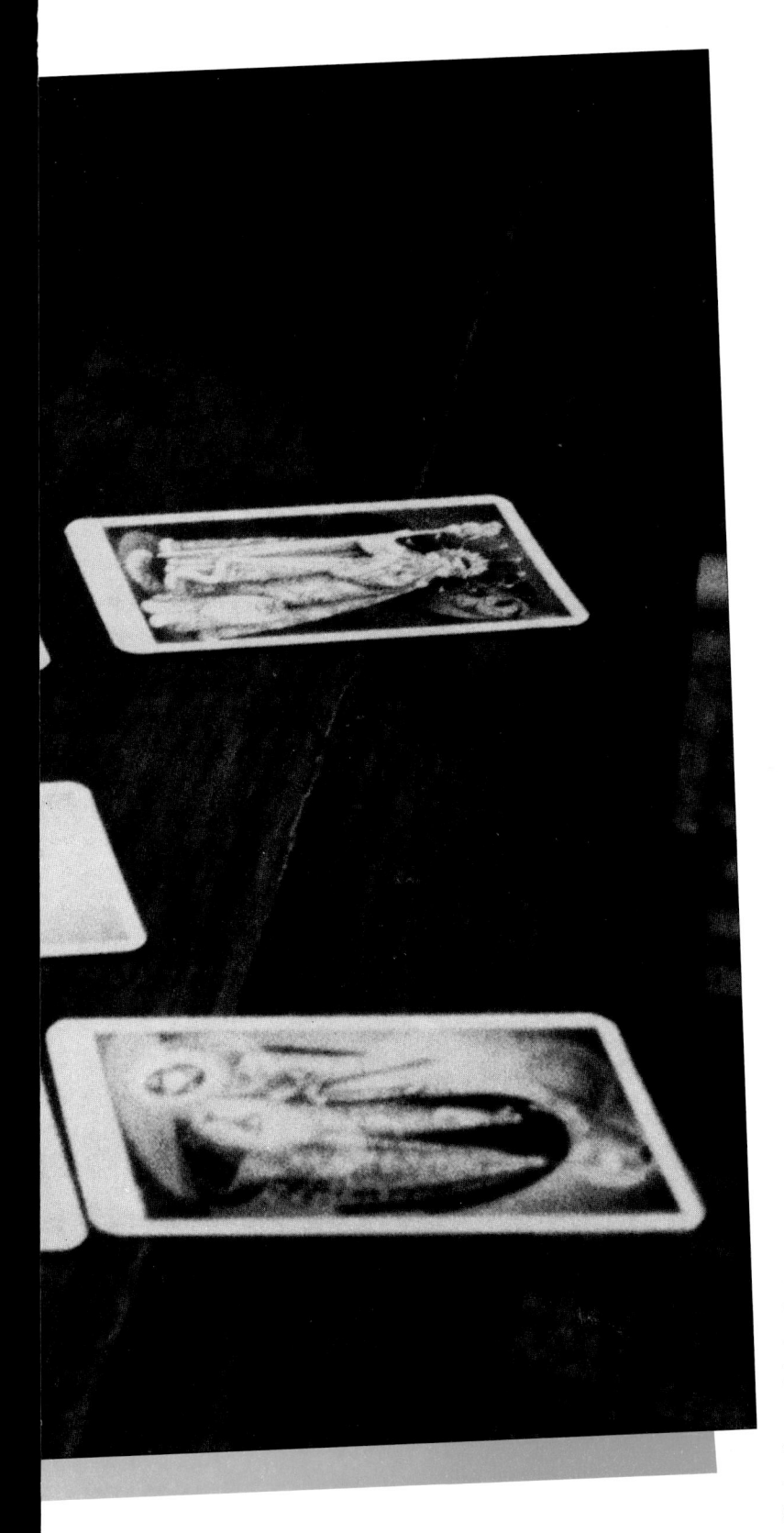

A London psychic lays out tarot cards in one of the many formations used in divination.

caul, a fetal membrane that covered his face. In several cultures the caul signifies second sight. Like most psychics, Tanous believes his gifts were manifest in childhood. Retrocognition was one of them. In school, he did well in history, he says, because he was able to return in time and relive whatever period was under study.

Among the most intriguing of Tanous's seeming paranormal aspects is the special relationship he claims to have with light. He energizes himself psychically, he says, by looking into bright lights, even into the sun. Although he recommends against others trying the technique, he reports that he himself has never suffered the retinal burns that might be expected to result. Moreover, Tanous's mysterious connection with light apparently encompasses transmitting as well as receiving. He can, according to some witnesses, make balls of light shoot out of his eyes.

Such extravagant claims meet considerable skepticism, of course. Nor are New Age paths to enlightenment always viewed with equanimity. The critics' responses range from mild to vitriolic. Some psychologists see the movement as a fairly innocuous attempt by people who are disillusioned with organized religion to fill a spiritual vacuum in their lives. "Many well-educated people have moved away from traditional religion," says Dr. Robert Millman of Cornell Medical College, an expert in social psychiatry. "But they still want to believe there is a force that is higher than themselves; they don't want to think they are insignificant little animals, produced by a random series of events. They want to know that there is a system, and they want to know where they fit in." Others, those who are wary of the cultlike aspect of some New Age phenomena, regard the movement as far more dangerous. A West German psychologist, describing an "occult epidemic" in his country, says teenagers are suffering mental health problems from contact with occult practices.

In one reported case in the United States, belief in a psychic's prediction proved deadly to a susceptible adult. A Colorado woman, upon being told by a medium that she and a married man for whom she cared would become lovers

Is This the Real You?

You are basically a serious person, but with a fine sense of humor. A loner by temperament, you nevertheless have a talent for working with others. You prefer people whose intellects equal yours, but you are never unkind to inferiors. You are very sensitive but tend to maintain a stiff upper lip in difficult times. You sometimes feel insecure, but you mask it so well that friends see you as confident and outgoing. You are meticulous — a perfectionist — but an overabundance of details bores you. You crave adventure but are never irresponsible. You have a complex nature and wide-ranging interests, coupled with a great ability to focus all your energies on a single task.

Does this description fit you? It should. It fits most people; or, at least, it fits the self-image of most people. Hardly anyone with a well-integrated ego cares to think of himself or herself as a frivolous, humorless, ignorant, insensitive, weak, boring, shallow clod. Any good psychic reader knows this; thus, a so-called cold reading — such as the one you just read — will almost always be flattering as well as general. It will also offer choices. Note that most of the propositions paired above are basically contradictory. Nevertheless, a psychic's client — generally known as a sitter — will tend to integrate them into a coherent statement. Moreover, the more intelligent the sitter, the more complete this integration is apt to be. Humans process all sensory input by imposing order on chaos, and they will usually react to a psychic reading no differently. And if you come down on one side of a reader's equation harder than on the other, well and good. Verbally or with body language, you will probably give the psychic enough clues to move from generalities to particulars.

Also operating in this situation is a phenomenon called subjective validation. This means that you tend to make the reader's statements fit in with what you already know or believe about yourself. In this way, the sitter may do most of the real work in a reading, interpreting the adviser's vague generalities as personally tailored revelations.

---

in a future life, killed the man and then committed suicide. Much criticism centers on speculation about fraud. "A lot of people get in to make money and pass themselves off as having supernatural powers," says Marc Medoff, publisher of *Whole Life* magazine, which deals with New Age topics. "We get complaints all the time from people who are charged a lot for rubbish that's made up on the spot." Jacob Needleman, a theologian at the University of California at Berkeley, notes there is "no Better Business Bureau" in the psychic world. "Let the buyer beware," he says. "You should be open-minded, but not so open-minded that your brains fall out."

In the main, the New Age is anathema to conventional religion. Some religious leaders see it as a kind of collective antichrist. Others simply deplore its depersonalization of God, with the concomitant notion that "anything is permissible if everything is God." "When people stop believing in God, they'll believe in anything," says Reverend Monsignor William B. Smith, academic dean and professor of moral theology at St. Joseph's Seminary in Yonkers, New York. "We start relying on ersatz substitutes: crystal balls, tarot cards. One is as irrational as the next, and none can determine your free will or your future." Even so, a New Age influence can be discerned in mainstream religion: an upswing in faith healing among Episcopalians, a revival of Jewish mysticism, the training of meditation in Roman Catholic monasteries.

It is doubtful that the New Age, in all its varied aspects, would have won unqualified approval from its precursors. Edgar Cayce and Eileen Garrett probably would have applauded the search for spiritual elevation. But, without question, Cayce would have been appalled by the New Age departure from traditional religion and the enthusiastic neopaganism. As for Eileen Garrett, Eileen Coley said her mother would have regarded much of the New Age as "utter nonsense."

Nevertheless, it was one of Mrs. Garrett's fondest hopes that her own work with psychic phenomena would hasten the time when people would find practical uses for such powers. Perhaps she would have been gratified to know that as the New Age dawned, pragmatists both within it and outside it were trying to do exactly that.

Psychics at Center Stage

The title psychic has been given to a diverse collection of characters, from medieval soothsayers to the unlettered Edgar Cayce. But nowhere has the word aroused more ire than in the field of stage magic. Professional magicians, or conjurers, usually have individual specialties. Illusionists cause large objects to appear or vanish (or so it seems); escape artists free themselves from seemingly inextricable bonds. Mentalists, the psychics of the stage, perform feats of apparent telepathy or clairvoyance, but some outrage fellow entertainers by claiming to have real psychic powers.

When believers in psychic phenomena point to these performers as living evidence of the paranormal, skeptics — many of them professional magicians — retort that mentalists such as Uri Geller and George Kresge, known as Kreskin, are nothing more than glorified tricksters, exploiting a gullible public. For their part, mentalists take a philosophical view: Just because psychic powers resist laboratory testing or can be copied by clever magicians is no reason to believe that such phenomena do not exist. The controversy began more than a century ago — and is not likely to end soon.

The Mind Who Came to Dinner

On May 12, 1889, a pale young man stood before a gathering at the exclusive Lambs Club of New York City. His goal: nothing less than to provide conclusive proof of his ability to read minds. Yet, despite supposed psychic gifts that had attracted worldwide attention, the thirty-three-year-old mentalist apparently did not foresee that this demonstration, the crowning event of his career, would have a gruesome finale.

Washington Irving Bishop was not any stranger to controversy. In the early 1880s, he had created a sensation with his Blindfold Carriage Test, a dramatic demonstration of what he termed mental telegraphy. Donning a heavy black hood and taking the reins of a horse-drawn cart, Bishop led a mob of 500 news reporters and spectators on a wild ride through midtown Manhattan as he tracked down a hidden diamond brooch—solely, he said, by the power of thought. Later, on a headline-making tour of Europe, the mentalist apparently read the thoughts of the Prince of Wales in order to locate a gold sovereign coin concealed in the Duchess of Kent's silk stocking. On that same tour, however, the young performer found himself at odds with an established magician, John Nevil Maskelyne, who claimed Bishop was a trickster without genuine powers. After a heated exchange of accusations, Bishop thought it prudent to leave Britain.

Returning to the United States, Bishop met more opposition. In New York, a promi-

Just months before his death, mind reader Washington Irving Bishop flaunts the medals he claimed to have received from the crowned heads of Europe.

Magician Jean Eugène Robert-Houdin and son Emile perform a second-sight act in 1848.

nent newspaper editor published his own explanation of many of Bishop's most prized thought-reading effects. Bishop, said the editor, was nothing more than a glorified magician. Although the performer steadfastly maintained that his demonstrations were genuine, the accusation seriously tarnished his reputation and left him more determined than ever to prove himself a genuine psychic. The Lambs Club afforded him an opportunity to restore his good name. When a friend invited him to dine, Bishop knew that the evening would provide an ideal platform for his talents.

After the meal was finished, the Lambs Club members—many of whom were show people themselves—clamored for a demonstration of thought reading. Bishop happily obliged them. A high-strung, agitated performer, he fairly quivered as he announced that he would favor the assembly with an effect that he had recently exhibited for the tsar of Russia. Before leaving the room in the company of a club member, Bishop asked that an imaginary murder scene be enacted in his absence, complete with a killer, a victim, a weapon, and a witness. The chosen killer, whose identity Bishop would not know, was instructed to select a victim, then act out a crime of his own devising, and finally hide the weapon.

This was done, and the members called Bishop back into the room with his chaperone, who attested that the mind reader could not have heard or seen anything that occurred in his absence. The mentalist set to work with characteristic energy. Allowing a blindfold to be fastened over his eyes, he took the arm of a witness and began pacing furiously. To the astonishment of all, Bishop unhesitatingly identified the killer and victim and located the hidden murder weapon.

The feat won warm applause, but the mentalist was far from finished. By now Bishop's nerves seemed at the breaking point; trembling hands and ashen features attested to the enormous strain of his efforts, but he seemed determined to press on.

Clay Green, the Lambs Club secretary, volunteered to help Bishop in his next feat. Bishop asked Green to focus all his thought on a book listing Lambs Club members. When he could picture it clearly in his mind, Bishop instructed, Green was to select a name found in its pages.

Again donning his heavy blindfold, Bishop grasped the secretary by the arm and led him on a frantic dash through the building, knocking over tables and chairs until—still blindfolded—the mentalist laid his hands on the register book Green had envisioned.

This demonstration of thought reading won more enthusiastic applause from the observers, but Bishop was not finished. Holding up a hand for silence, the performer announced that he would reveal—by probing Green's innermost thoughts—the name selected moments earlier. Bishop still clutched Green by the arm. His features contorted with effort; a series of groans escaped his lips. Finally, his hands jerking spasmodically, he seized a pen and pad and scrawled a puzzling message:

ᗡ Ν Ǝ S N M O T

Nonplussed, Green revealed that he had chosen the name Margaret Townsend from the membership rolls. When he held the message up to a mirror, the name TOWNSEND was dramatically revealed.

Even as the audience exploded into applause, Bishop's exertions caught up with him. The performer pulled off his blindfold and crumpled to the floor. Stunned club members put him to bed in an upstairs room, and a doctor in attendance attempted to revive Bishop with electric shocks and injections of brandy. Not surprisingly, by the time morning arrived he was unconscious and was soon pronounced dead.

This was not the first time such a thing had happened to Bishop. The young man suffered from catalepsy, a condition characterized by sudden plunges into an unconsciousness so deep that all life signs were supressed. Often the stresses of his performances would bring seizures upon him. Indeed, Bishop had been pronounced dead on two previous occasions, only to recover unaided several hours later.

There would be no such recovery after the Lambs Club episode. Convinced that the mentalist was dead, a doctor from New York Hospital immediately performed an autopsy, removing his brain. Bishop's distraught mother arrived too late to prevent the action. Ever afterward she maintained that her son had been murdered by medical ghouls, eager to learn the secrets of Bishop's powers.

Trade Secrets

Ironically, the man who had risen to fame as "the world's first and world eminent mind reader" began his career as the scourge of spiritualism. In 1876, capitalizing on secrets learned as an assistant to Anna Eva Fay, a famous American medium, Bishop developed a popular stage program in which he re-created—and then exposed—the most cherished routines of professional mediums.

A feature of this act, and one that Bishop insisted was genuine, was a demonstration of thought reading. However, Bishop's thought-reading stunts, which he advanced as evidence of superior powers, took their inspiration from a world-renowned magician—a man who made no claim whatsoever to psychic gifts.

Jean Eugène Robert-Houdin, a French clockmaker turned conjurer, had stunned Parisian audiences in the 1840s with his seemingly supernatural second-sight act. His performance was straightforward enough, but it had a dazzling effect. While the magician circulated among his audience, his young son Emile sat blindfolded on the stage. As audience members handed Robert-Houdin small items from their pockets or handbags, the magician asked his son to identify them. Emile would then shout out astonishingly complete descriptions, as if—though blindfolded—he could plainly see the objects. No detail escaped the magician's son; he could even be counted on to recite the contents of private letters or read the foreign-language inscriptions on medallions and coins that were proffered.

The second-sight act, which relied on an ingenious and elaborate verbal code understood only by the magician and his son, proved ill-suited to the plans of Washington Irving Bishop, who preferred to work alone. Accordingly, Bishop traded the secrets he gleaned from Robert-Houdin's memoirs to a resourceful mentalist named J. Randall Brown. In return, Brown taught Bishop the technique that would come to make him famous. Brown's technique, known today as muscle reading, is itself very nearly as incredible as the seemingly psychic feats it enabled Bishop to perform. Only a handful of mentalists over the last century have mastered this delicate, inexact skill, which depends on unconscious physical indicators given by an innocent volunteer. In a typical case, the performer of muscle reading will ask his subject, usually a member of the audience, to concentrate on an object hidden nearby. Then, gripping the arm or wrist of the subject, the muscle reader begins to move about the room, asking for mental commands leading to the hidden object, such as "go forward" or "turn left."

With enough practice, the performer becomes sensitive to tiny movements by the subject that are imperceptible to the audience. For example, if the subject gives a slight pulse of resistance, the performer realizes he is heading the wrong way. If there is no resistance, the direction is correct. Thus, even when blindfolded, a stage mentalist using this technique can locate a hidden object as long as he is touching someone who knows where the object is. A canny performer can very easily give the appearance of reading minds.

Bishop relied heavily on muscle reading as he molded himself into one of the nineteenth century's most remarkable performers. So great was his success that by the time of his unfortunate death in 1889, public exhibitions of thought reading had become almost commonplace.

Psychics under the Big Top

Although Bishop's career had ended, the public's appetite for demonstrations of psychic powers remained very much alive. A host of colorful Bishop imitators emerged in

Eleanor Bishop hovers over the lifeless body of her son, who by 1889 had become the world's foremost thought reader. An autopsy line across the deceased mentalist's forehead attests to the unfortunate circumstances of his death.

A lithograph advertises the young Harry Houdini's skill as a card manipulator without mentioning the mentalism act that the magician sometimes performed on the same bill.

Despite his success, Houdini remained ambivalent about his career as a mentalist. In 1898, he decided to abandon the act, claiming that if he could not make good as a real magician within a year, he would find himself a more respectable job.

Anna Eva Fay, considered the greatest female stage psychic of all time, shared none of Houdini's reservations about her chosen career. Fay was an accomplished magician who turned to mentalism in the 1870s, giving séances in music halls and variety shows. By the time of her retirement in 1924, she had risen to the status of a vaudeville headliner. Described as "a slender, almost fragile creature with grey eyes and flaxen hair," the psychic invariably made a most bewildering impression on her audiences.

In the centerpiece of Fay's act, the mentalist sat on the stage, blindfolded and covered by a thick orange sheet, as she answered unspoken questions from the audience. At the start of every performance, she explained that in order for her to form a clear psychic impression, each question must be written out on a pad of paper. Participants then ripped off the top sheet and Fay's assistants collected the unused portion of the pads. Almost immediately, the mentalist would begin calling out answers from beneath her sheet.

Ironically, it was Washington Irving Bishop, a former assistant, who exposed her ingenious secret—though her career seemed unaffected by Bishop's revelations. In an the 1890s, many of them magicians whose careers had hit the skids. These performers, of widely varying skill and credibility, permeated the circuses, "dime museums," and variety halls of the day, often vanishing from public view as quickly as they had appeared. Those who managed to duplicate Bishop's effects could seldom match his attention-grabbing histrionics—except perhaps for Theodore Pull, whose gimmick of chewing on a piece of soap during his performances gave the impression that psychic fervor caused him to foam at the mouth.

Even Harry Houdini, later the most vehement antispiritualist of his generation, served a brief early turn as a psychic entertainer. Known at the turn of the century as Dime Museum Harry, owing to the seedy venues in which he appeared, Houdini brought the same flair to his mind-reading act that he would later apply to his career as an escape artist. Transmitting coded signals to his wife, Bess, with almost imperceptible wiggles of his right ear, Houdini could stage a convincing display of mentalism. When, on one occasion, he appeared to be delivering messages from a local murder victim, superstitious audience members fled from the theater in panic.

Magician James S. Harto — also known as Chandra — and his wife, Verda Wren, affected exotic silk robes to capitalize on the demand for mystical thought-reading acts.

84

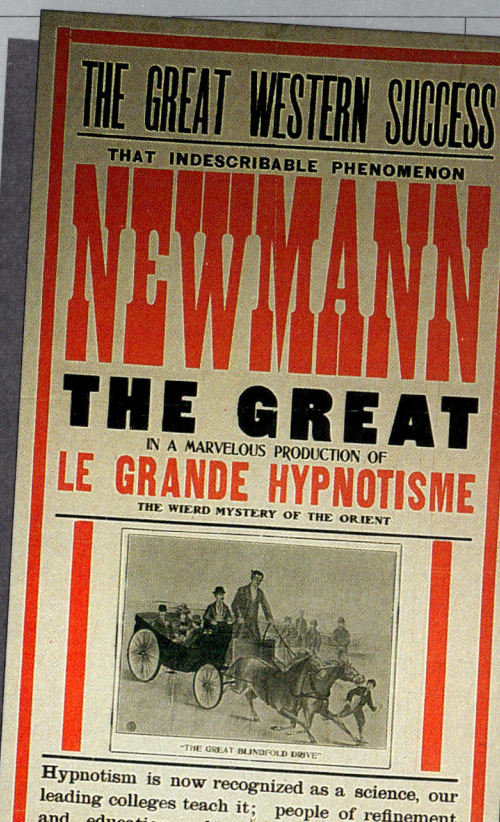

anonymous newspaper article published early in both performers' careers, Bishop revealed that as Fay's spectators wrote their questions on the note pads provided, a thin coating of paraffin on the second sheet took an impression of the pencil markings. Backstage, her assistants quickly dusted the paraffin with graphite, yielding a clear copy of the questions while the originals remained in the hands of the audience. The assistants then transmitted these questions to Fay through a speaking tube that ran through a hole drilled in the stage floor.

Having taken such extraordinary measures to discern her audience's questions, Fay was scarcely less clever in devising the answers. Generally the questions held simple pleas for advice, but Fay proved herself equal to greater challenges. On one occasion late in her career, a Brooklyn man asked where his stolen car might be found. Pausing dramatically and giving appropriate gasps of effort from beneath her orange covering, the performer slowly recited an address. The next day's newspapers reported that the missing automobile had indeed been found at that exact location. As the city buzzed with the news of Fay's stunning feat, an energetic reporter uncovered a disillusioning piece of information. Fay's husband had paid two men to steal the car and park it in a prearranged location. Simple theft, not psychic illumination, had brought about the miracle.

Such revelations did little to dampen the public's enthusiasm for mentalism on the stage. Another stage psychic, Stuart Cumberland, claimed that more than 1,000 scientists and members of the clergy had endorsed his powers as genuine. Along with thought reading, Cumberland regaled his audiences with tales of having read the best minds of the era, including those of British statesman William E. Gladstone and Kaiser Wilhelm II of Germany.

Even Fannie Brice, the popular comedic star of the Ziegfeld Follies, was known to entertain her friends with amateur mind-reading stunts. Asked for an explanation, she replied, rather obliquely, "Oh, I just do these things, darling."

Minds of the Times

As the demand grew for psychic entertainment, the techniques used by Bishop and others became more widely known to the public. Audiences familiar with codes and muscle reading demanded more sophisticated feats before they would consider a psychic genuine.

Maude Lancaster, an English woman, demonstrated one great procedural improvement. In 1893, while performing the familiar stunt of locating a hidden object, Lancaster succeeded without physical contact of any kind. Although blindfolded, she also duplicated Bishop's murder-mystery test and several other impressive stunts, all without benefit of touch.

Lancaster's success prompted many to proclaim her a genuine psychic, but in fact she was one of the first to use a technique that soon came to be called noncontact thought reading. This method of achieving seemingly psychic results relied mainly on a keen visual interpretation of the same physical clues felt by the earlier muscle readers.

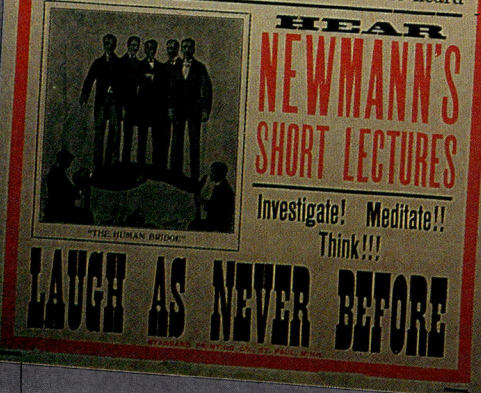

C. A. George Newmann performed his act in a way that confounded all as to the secret of his blindfold carriage ride. As shown here, he gripped the horses' reins, not his volunteer's wrist.

Joseph Mercedes and Mademoiselle Stantone combined thought reading with piano playing in a "mental novelty" act one critic called "the acme of finesse."

To be successful with this highly delicate approach, a performer needed sharp eyes, hours of practice, and—in many cases—a see-through blindfold.

C. A. George Newmann may have had all of these things and more. The Minnesota-bred mentalist, whose long career spanned the years from the late 1890s into the 1950s, even one-upped Washington Irving Bishop's famous blindfolded carriage rides. Unlike his predecessor, who took the reins in one hand and the wrist of his helper in the other, Newmann would keep both hands on the reins of his carriage, while the person who had hidden the search object remained in the back seat. Even if he was aided by the noncontact technique, it seems as if Newmann must have had eyes in the back of his head to succeed in this dramatic display; his secret has never been revealed to the public.

Not all stage mentalists relied on such techniques. A phenomenal act from the 1920s and 1930s called "Mercedes and the Marvelous Musical Mystic Mademoiselle Stantone" had its roots in the verbal deception of the illustrious Robert-Houdin. In this act, Joseph Mercedes moved among his audience, encouraging spectators to whisper the names of popular tunes into his ear. Almost at once, the blindfolded Mademoiselle Stantone, seated at a piano on stage, would play the chosen selections.

This act fooled not only the pair's vast audiences but also magicians familiar with Robert-Houdin's word code. The performers spoke very little during their act, and what they said varied only slightly from night to night. Could this at last be a demonstration of actual psychic power on stage?

The solution proved less mystical, though nearly as impressive. Rather than rely on a spoken code, Mercedes had devised a system based on the length of the pauses between his words to communicate the selected tunes. Thus, even while Mademoiselle Stantone played a brisk fox trot or languorous waltz, the two performers remained synchronized by a private tempo counted off silently to themselves.

Stage mentalists continued to entrance audiences through the first decades of the twentieth century, even as the exact nature of their art grew more controversial. No two figures more clearly embodied the opposing sides of that debate than the distinguished writer Sir Arthur Conan Doyle, an avid spiritualist, and the zealously skeptical Harry

The thought-transference act of Julius Zancig and his wife, Agnes, impressed even Houdini, who admitted "I have failed to trace anyone superior."

Houdini. Although fast friends, the two men found themselves at odds over the mind-reading capabilities of Danish performers Julius and Agnes Zancig.

In an act entitled "Two Minds with a Single Thought," Zancig and his wife appeared to read each other's mind as well as minds in the audience. The pair generated such interest that within a few years of their debut in 1892 they commanded the most exclusive stages in show business, including an eleven-week engagement at Oscar Hammerstein's famed Roof Garden in New York City. One journalist was so moved by the Zancigs' seeming ability to read and transmit thoughts that he wrote: "It is a case of telepathy pure and simple. The respective mental batteries of this pair are so perfectly adjusted that the vibration of the thought current of the man instantly registers itself upon the mind of the wife."

Conan Doyle echoed this opinion. After seeing the Zancigs' act in 1922, the creator of Sherlock Holmes commented: "I am quite assured that their remarkable performance, as I saw it, was due to psychic causes [thought transference] and not to trickery."

The British author, renowned for the rigid logic and keen reasoning of his fictional detective, was an uncritical supporter of psychic claims, and he spent the final years of his life in enthusiastic pursuit of paranormal phenomena. In his passion, Conan Doyle would often proclaim mediums and psychics to be genuine even when other observers could easily provide more mundane explanations of their feats.

Houdini, despite his own early turn as a mentalist, had become the world's foremost exposer of fraudulent mediums, tirelessly attending performances and séances in order to confront phony spiritualists. In fact, many of the conjurer's own performances were given over to the exposure of mediums whom he believed to be bilking the public of hard-earned money.

In his book *A Magician among the Spirits*, Houdini commented on Conan Doyle's fascination with the Zancigs: "Mr. Julius Zancig is a magician, a member of the Society of American Magicians of which I have been the President for the past seven years. I believe he is one of the greatest second-sight artists that magical history records. It would not be fair to disclose his methods despite the fact that Sir Arthur Conan Doyle put the stamp of genuineness on his work. Undoubtedly it *appeared* unfathomable to Sir Arthur and he therefore concluded that it was psychic and that there could be no other solution." Houdini's comments undoubtedly failed to shake Conan Doyle's conviction, for the author also believed that Houdini himself possessed psychic powers enabling him to perform his astonishing escapes and illusions — an idea strenuously rejected by the magician.

In any event, the question of the Zancigs was decisively resolved two years later when Julius Zancig, who was badly down on his luck, was forced to sell off the secret of his second-sight act — an ingenious verbal code — to a London newspaper.

The Man with the X-Ray Eyes

Unique among performing mentalists, Kuda Bux — "The Man with the X-Ray Eyes" — managed to excite the interest of psychic investigators without raising the ire of magicians. Born in Kashmir, India, in 1905, Bux first gained notoriety for walking across blazing coals or paraffin without suffering harm—a skill that he had mastered as a youth. By 1935, the stoical performer had been tested with a stroll across a fire measured at 1,400 degrees centigrade. However, after he emigrated to the United States in the late 1930s, Bux became better known for feats of so-called eyeless sight. His stage act raised simple blindfold effects to a level that may never be surpassed—or explained.

Bux disdained the use of plain cloth blindfolds. When he performed, he insisted that there be no possibility of "sneaking a peek." First, under the mentalist's instruction, audience members fastened large coins over each eyeball with adhesive tape. Then other spectators pushed masses of flour paste into both eye sockets, followed by cotton wads and more tape. Finally, they wound a wide surgical bandage around Bux's head. Not only did this lengthy process seemingly deprive the mentalist of his sight, but it added a drama to his appearance on stage. Bux asked only that no one plug up his nostrils, a stipulation that prompted one psychic researcher to ask, perfectly seriously, "Can anybody see with his nostrils?"

Even so encumbered, Bux was able to copy written messages, read books, and describe objects held up by the audience. On one occasion, he rode a bicycle through New York's Times Square in heavy traffic, an impressive feat even without the blindfold.

Bux delighted in misleading the press about the source and extent of his eyeless sight. Once, after dazzling a reporter with his various stunts while blindfolded, Bux made an elaborate show of looking for his glasses—without them, he explained, he was helpless. Similarly, Bux claimed: "If I am blindfolded, I don't make mistakes. But if I close my eyes I make the same mistakes as other people—I collide with objects." These statements delighted and bemused Bux's many magician friends, who would agree to play a game of cards with him only after they had laid down a strict rule: The mentalist was not permitted to wear his blindfold.

Many researchers and magicians were at a loss to explain Bux's abilities. The mystery deepened when, after a cataract operation damaged his vision, Bux continued to perform his act with the same clear-eyed results.

Perhaps the greatest tribute to Bux's skills came, quite unintentionally, from three female singers with whom he once made a tour of Britain. Assigned to a dressing room next door to Bux's, the women threatened to break their contract. The reason: "We would have no privacy. There is only one brick wall between us and Kuda Bux."

Horse Sense

In the 1920s, a psychic phenomenon of a very different kind captured the imagination of the public. Lady Wonder, the so-called educated mind-reading horse, was by no means the first animal to rise to psychic prominence. In

Although swathed beneath layers of gauze, tape, and sticky paste, Kashmiri mentalist Kuda Bux remained able to read books and to ride a bicycle, living up to his billing as "the Man with the X-Ray Eyes."

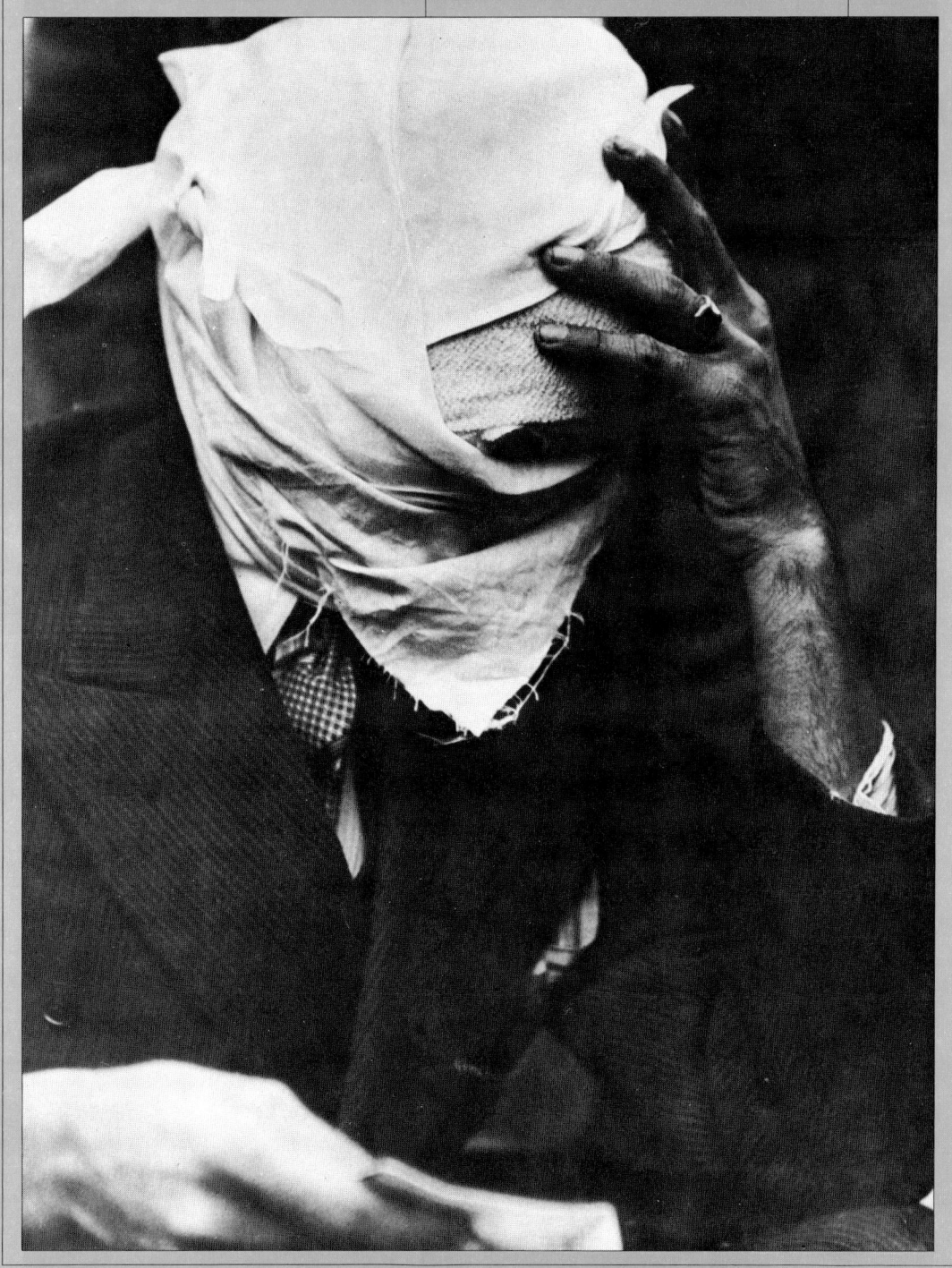

Lady Wonder's calling card (above) invites visitors to the horse's Virginia stable. For one dollar, the animal would answer questions using a keyboard (left).

1817, Toby, the Sapient Pig, startled Londoners by correctly indicating numbers and words thought of by his audiences. Geese, goats, seals, and even rats have all taken to the stage to perform seemingly telepathic acts. Yet Lady Wonder, whose stamping grounds were just outside Richmond, Virginia, was perhaps the first to warrant a full-scale psychic investigation.

The remarkable horse and her owner, Claudia Fonda, never traveled the show-business circuit. Instead, interested observers visited them at Lady Wonder's stable, where the animal stood poised behind an outsize typewriter, ready to peck out answers to questions by nudging the keys with her nose. For more than twenty-five years, Lady Wonder made headlines by predicting the outcomes of national elections, ball games, and—perhaps somewhat less surprisingly—horse races.

In 1927, the noted parapsychologist Joseph Banks Rhine went to Richmond to test the psychic horse. At first, Rhine found himself amazed by the horse's gifts. But after subjecting Lady Wonder to tests similar to those he applied to human subjects, he came to suspect that she was responding to subtle physical cues from her owner.

In separate tests that he conducted some years later, the magician Milbourne Christopher reached the same conclusion. According to Christopher, a luminary in the world of magic as both a performer and a historian, the horse's predictions of future events could be chalked up to Mrs. Fonda's knowledge of current events and the propensity of the public to forget incorrect prophecies.

Lady Wonder herself remained quite unspooked by the controversy. As late as 1956, the horse continued to make—and predict—newspaper headlines.

Lady Wonder was only one among many mentalist performers to submit to psychic testing. In the 1930s, stage mentalists and average citizens alike came under the scrutiny of British mathematician Samuel George Soal in his quest to solve the mystery of mental telepathy. By 1939, Soal had conducted more than 120,000 tests on 140 people of varied background and education.

Mentalist under the Microscope

Easily the most unusual of Soal's subjects was a popular stage performer by the name of Frederick Marion. Born in Prague, Czechoslovakia, Marion was an adept entertainer who could locate hidden objects in a flash, even amid the most impenetrable clutter. The mentalist scored unusually well

Mentalist Frederick Marion holds his hand over face-down playing cards in a 1934 experiment. Marion was trying to probe the mind of Dr. S. G. Soal (left foreground) for the location of a preselected card.

88

in Soal's standard battery of ESP tests, but the researcher, familiar with the methods of other performers, had a suspicion that Marion was actually practicing noncontact thought reading. To test this theory, Soal built a heavy wooden device he called a sentry box for the psychic researchers to stand in during their experiments. The device restricted body movements, thereby limiting the physical signals that Soal and his assistants might unconsciously transmit to Marion. The box also shielded them from Marion's view while allowing the mentalist the voice and eye contact he required.

According to Soal, who published a report entitled *Preliminary Studies of a Vaudeville Telepathist,* Marion lost his ability to find hidden objects when his testers were shielded within the sentry box.

Still, such skills as muscle reading could not account for all of Marion's success, nor could the laboratory contain all of his feats. The performer frequently amazed his audiences with his ability to reconstruct past events from the lives of total strangers, based only on a half-dozen random words jotted on a slip of paper.

Marion related the story of how, during one such demonstration held at a large hall in London in 1934, a small, sharp-featured woman rose from the audience and accused the mentalist of employing confederates. She was Margot, Lady Oxford and Asquith, wife of the former prime minister of England. The mentalist quickly rose to the challenge. Inviting his critic to join him on stage, Marion asked Lady Asquith to concentrate on an important event from her past. Then he requested a random sample of her handwriting, which he had her seal away in a plain envelope.

Closing his eyes, Marion began to speak. "There is a large room," he said, "with bookshelves lining some of the walls. In this room, a man is sitting behind a huge table. A number of documents are spread on the table in front of him. He is reading something. He picks up a pen, then puts it down and rises from his seat to walk up and down the room. Returning to his seat, he once again picks up the pen. As he does so, a door behind him opens slightly. Somebody is looking into the room. The man writes, then takes a handkerchief from his pocket and dabs his eyes. He is crying."

Here a gasp from Lady Asquith halted the performer's narrative. Trembling, she turned to the audience and acknowledged that Marion had indeed read her private thoughts. She said: "The room Marion describes is the study of Number Ten Downing Street. The incident occurred there in August of 1914. At the moment Marion describes, my husband was in the act of signing the declaration of war against Germany."

Seeing Through the Iron Curtain

In 1910, a penniless eleven-year-old Polish boy boarded a train bound for Berlin, beginning a psychic career that would draw in such figures as Hitler, Stalin, Einstein, and Freud. As the grown psychic would later tell the story, the boy crouched under a seat that day in 1910, hoping to escape the notice of the ticket collector. When the conductor demanded to see his ticket, the boy, acting on a fearful impulse, handed him a worthless piece of paper torn from a newspaper.

"Our glances met," he later recounted, "and with all my strength I willed that he would take that piece of paper as a ticket."

Following a long pause, the conductor punched the piece of paper as he would an ordinary ticket and handed it back to the boy saying, "Why are you hiding under the seat if you have a perfectly good ticket?"

Wolf Messing claimed that this was his first experience of his remarkable powers of telepathic projection, or, in his words, the ability to cloud men's minds. It would be some time, however, before Messing learned to put his abilities to use. The performer later recounted how he wandered the streets of Berlin for days without food or shelter, finally succumbing to a cataleptic fit, the very condition that had plagued Washington Irving Bishop two decades earlier.

Fortunately, although Messing's body grew cold and stiff, the doctors who were

S. G. Soal demonstrates his so-called sentry box, devised to limit the unconscious physical signals he could transmit to Marion. By adding or removing wooden panels, Soal controlled how much of his body the mentalist could see.

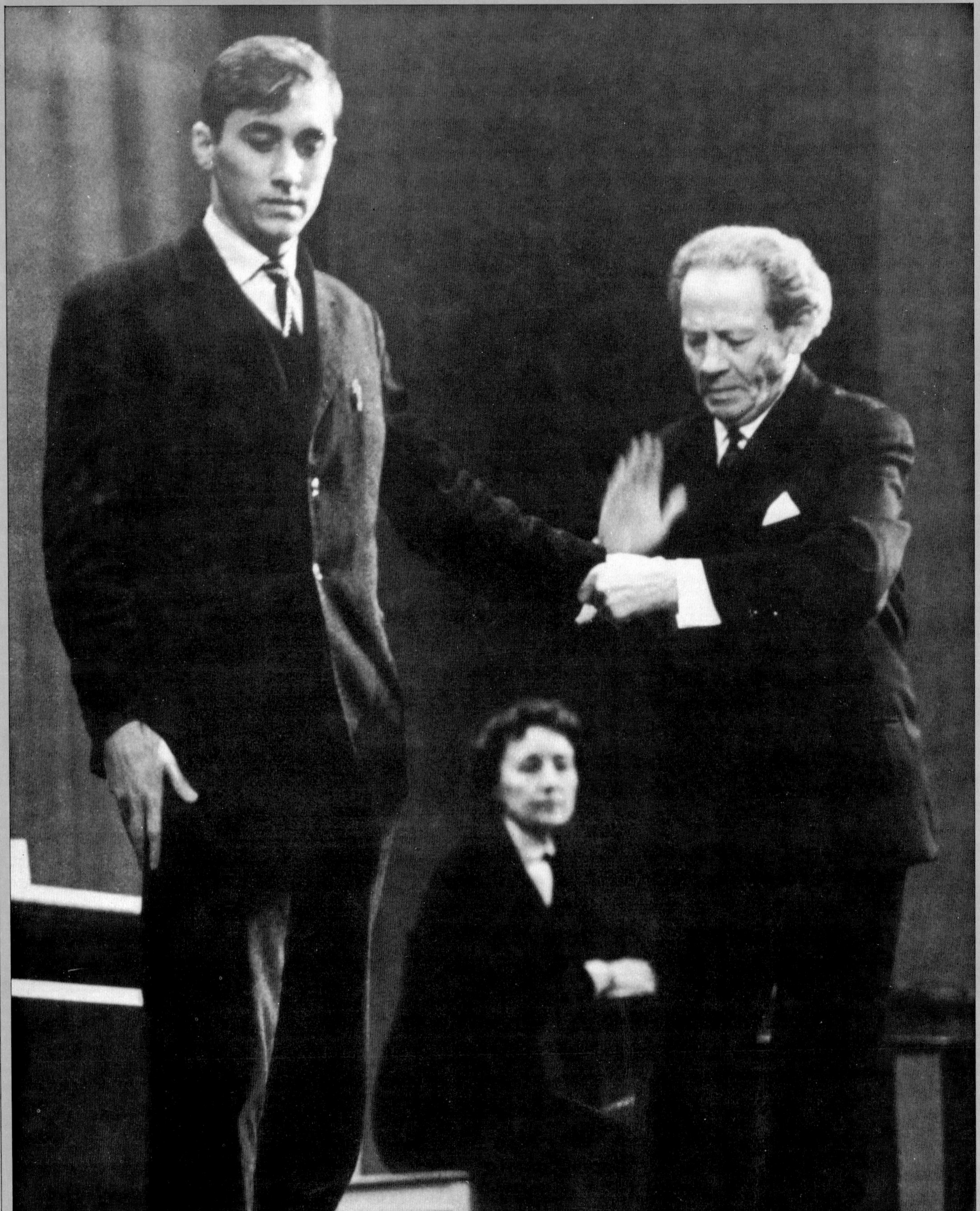

attending the stricken boy detected a faint heartbeat just as he was being dispatched to the morgue, thus sparing him the fate of his predecessor. His catalepsy brought him good fortune, however, in that it led to his first show-business job: lying motionless in a crystal casket at the Berlin waxworks, on display as a "living corpse."

By the age of sixteen, Messing had developed a mind-reading and so-called miracle-detective act in Berlin, in which he located valuables hidden among the audience. In this way, Messing came before two of the most famous, if amateur, psychic researchers of all time.

After a performance in Vienna, Messing recounted, he was invited to the apartment of thirty-six-year-old Albert Einstein. Ushering Messing into his study, Einstein introduced the teen-age entertainer to a visiting friend, Sigmund Freud, the founder of psychoanalysis. Freud insisted on testing Messing's mind-reading ability. The young Pole happily agreed to attempt a probe of the Viennese doctor's consciousness.

As Messing concentrated his energy, however, a look of consternation spread across his face. It was not that he could not fathom Freud's unspoken message, Messing said later; he simply could not believe it. Finally, with a shrug, the mentalist went to Einstein's bathroom cupboard and took out a pair of tweezers. Returning to Einstein, Messing hesitantly explained that Freud wished him to pluck three hairs from the physicist's mustache. Smiling, Einstein proffered his upper lip and, Messing later claimed, the mentalist carried out his task.

In the years that followed, Messing's reputation spread throughout the world. The thought reader performed in such places as Japan, Brazil, Switzerland, Italy, and India, where he claimed to have successfully read the thoughts of Mahatma Gandhi.

In Poland, Messing was able to find more work as a "miracle detective," placing his services at the disposal of the police force. One of the notable cases that Messing claimed to have solved involved a Count Czartoryski, a member of a wealthy and powerful Polish family. The theft of the Count's heirloom jewels had left the police baffled. As a last resort, the Count flew Messing to his castle in a private airplane.

The performer recounted how he probed the castle grounds with his mind, soon coming to suspect the young son of one of the Count's servants. Inspecting the child's room, Messing found himself drawn to an enormous stuffed bear, which he snatched up and presented to the nobleman. When the bear was cut open, the missing jewels spilled forth, along with worthless bits of colored glass and other shiny objects. Evidently the boy had a fascination with glittering objects and hid any he came across inside the stuffing of his toy.

Overcome with gratitude, Count Czartoryski offered Messing a large reward. Messing refused, asking instead for a favor. The mentalist, who was Jewish, supposedly requested that the Count use his considerable political influence to help abolish a law infringing on the rights of Poland's Jews. The Count readily agreed, and within two weeks, Messing claimed, the law was repealed.

Messing was living in Poland when Hitler's army invaded in September of 1939. Two years earlier, before an audience of 1,000 people, Messing had predicted that Hitler would die if his armies turned east. Supposedly, news of the prophesy reached the führer, and he placed a price of 200,000 marks on Messing's head. As the German forces swept into the country, Messing fled.

The performer crossed into the Soviet Union hidden in a wagonload of hay. As a Jewish immigrant and practicing psychic, Messing's prospects in Stalin's Russia were poor. Yet, within three years, Messing rose to a position of prominence.

Messing's remarkable career in the Soviet Union began on a grim note in the city of Gomel. The mentalist later told how, in the midst of a sellout performance, two uniformed KGB officers stalked onto the stage, halted the proceedings, and dragged Messing off to a waiting car. After a long, anxious ride and a thorough search of his person, Messing found himself face to face with none other than Joseph Stalin.

The Soviet leader, apparently interested in Messing's gifts, invented a test of the mentalist's telepathic powers. Posing as an ordinary customer, Messing was to enter a Moscow bank and present the teller with a blank slip of paper. Then, by projecting his thoughts, Messing had to convince the teller to cash the blank slip as a check for 100,000 rubles.

The task, Messing asserted, went off without a hitch. He said that the elderly teller whom he approached looked at the blank slip (which had been torn out of an old school notebook), opened the bank's vault, and counted out the money. Later, when Messing returned the currency, the bewildered teller examined the blank slip, looked at Messing in disbelief, and fell to the floor with a heart attack. "Luckily," Messing wrote, "it wasn't fatal."

Messing reported that, impressive as his demonstration was, it did not entirely satisfy Stalin, who proposed an even more difficult test. The Soviet leader owned a heavily guarded house in the country. If Messing had the ability to cloud men's minds, then surely he could slip past Stalin's secret police. Messing agreed to try.

The mentalist recounted that a few days afterward, as Stalin was working at his desk, he looked up to see Messing stroll casually through the door, having telepathically persuaded Stalin's guards that he was the head of the Soviet secret police. Stalin required no further tests.

Was Messing blessed with genuine psychic powers, or was he the most successful conjurer and self-promoter of modern history? Ludmila Svinka-Zielinski, a foreign correspondent who followed Messing's exploits, held that for the mentalist to have prospered under the constant scrutiny of the Soviet Union, he could not have dared fraud or even vain boasts. "To exist in the environment on such a level," she wrote, "Wolf Messing must be thoroughly authentic."

Messing himself waxed philosophical on the subject: "The time is coming," he once said, "when man will understand these phenomena. There is nothing strange, only what is not yet commonplace."

Radio's Mastermind

Even as Wolf Messing solidified his reputation behind the Iron Curtain, another colorful entertainer was stirring amazement in the United States. The son of poor German immigrants, Joseph Dunninger often claimed that his fate was sealed when, at the age of seven, he was taken to see a performance by Harry Kellar, one of the world's great magicians. Within a year, "Master Joseph Dunninger, Child Magician" had secured a booking at a Masonic lodge in New York. By the age of sixteen he was performing sleight-of-hand acts, and for the next ten years he seemed destined to pursue the career of a stage magician, without any particular emphasis on feats of mentalism.

In 1917, however, the twenty-five-year-old conjurer's career hit a turning point. To draw attention to the opening of his illusion show in Hartford, Connecticut, Dunninger staged a well-publicized blindfolded automobile drive through the city, on his way to tracking down an object hidden by a com-

Wolf Messing (opposite, right), whose prophesies were said to strike fear into Adolf Hitler, demonstrates his thought-reading act with an audience volunteer at a state university in Moscow.

mittee of townspeople. By updating the blindfolded carriage rides of Washington Irving Bishop, Dunninger scored one of the greatest publicity coups of his career. From that point on, he devoted himself almost exclusively to mentalism.

Two years later, Dunninger presented himself to a crowd of news reporters at the Boston Press Club as the president of an apocryphal organization called the American Psychical Society. In this capacity, Dunninger professed to have conducted important research into the science of telepathy. In the future, he claimed, every man and woman on earth would become skilled at mind reading, with incalculable benefits for the human race: Police would know the plans of criminals as soon as they were made, doctors would conduct psychic examinations of their patients, and communication by telephone would become obsolete.

In order to confirm his "purely scientific" discovery, Dunninger offered a demonstration of these powers. Distributing sheets of paper, the mentalist asked each reporter present to jot down a name, number, or other significant item. Then he asked them all to fold the slips and give them to a volunteer. Dunninger tucked these papers into an empty envelope, sealed it, and threw it on the floor, instructing his volunteer to hold it under his foot.

Without another glance at the envelope, Dunninger took a seat across the room and—to the astonishment of all present—promptly read off the contents of the paper slips.

Before long, the Boston newspapers were filled with accounts of this and other Dunninger marvels. One story told of how he singled one person out of a crowd of 3,000 at the Boston Common after a committee had sealed away a written description of the man. Another item told how Dunninger stunned the editors of a prominent newspaper by spelling out a headline they had secretly selected from their vast files. Before long, the "brilliant young investigator," as one newspaper called him, was prevailed upon to give a public demonstration of his gifts. Thus began a quarter of a century of top theatrical billing for the performer.

In presenting himself as a genuine psychic, rather than as a magician performing mind-reading tricks, Dunninger incurred a predictable wave of wrath from some of his former peers. One magician even drew up sketches that showed Dunninger palming his audiences' slips of paper and reading them under the cover of a note pad. Dunninger denied the charge but revealed his ire by writing an article of his own that exposed the techniques of many other magicians. Eventually, the controversy led to Dunninger's expulsion from the National Conjuror's Association.

A promotional card emphasizes the dramatic appearance of Joseph Dunninger, who seemed to read minds over the airwaves.

By this time, however, Dunninger had become too successful to be damaged by a few accusations. Already a striking figure, the six-foot performer enhanced his dramatic image by growing out his thick black hair and sporting bright silk ties, a diamond stickpin, and white gloves and spats both on stage and off. He took his show across America, seeming to read the minds of contemporary notables such as Babe Ruth and Jack Dempsey. When not appearing in public, Dunninger commanded exorbitant fees at elite private functions given by such society figures as the Astors, the Tiffanys, and the Vanderbilts.

In 1943, the mentalist achieved even greater celebrity with an enormously popular weekly radio program. At 6:30 on Sunday evenings, Dunninger's voice would be heard apparently reading the minds of the studio audience. He heightened his effects through the clever use of telephone hookups and remote studios, creating the impression that he could read minds at any distance.

In the 1950s, Dunninger moved to television, which proved an even richer environment for his talents. With the aid of remote cameras, he seemed to divine the thoughts of people in distant, inaccessible locations, including those of a naval officer aboard a submarine and a parachutist plummeting to earth.

Although he had a standing invitation from Joseph Rhine, the performer never submitted to formal testing by psychic researchers. His promotional literature, however, spoke of an early test by no less a scientist than Thomas Edison, who was quoted as saying, "Never have I witnessed anything as mystifying or seemingly impossible."

His detractors doubted such claims. As Dunninger's fame grew, so too did the attacks from professional magicians. "Dunninger," one conjurer said bitterly, "can't read the mind of a gnat. The only thing he can project is baloney." To all such charges, Dunninger had an unvaried response: If these magicians knew how his act was done, they were free to duplicate it. "The Dunninger act," he asserted proudly, "is the only thing in magic that has never been copied—if it is magic!"

"Close Your Eyes, Merv, and Concentrate"

Although Dunninger meant to discourage imitators by these words, a young man from New Jersey took the challenge seriously. As a child, George Kresge had been fascinated by the popular comic strip *Mandrake the Magician*. By the age of eleven, he took to the stage with a hypnosis act—although, as he later admitted, "I think more people fell asleep in the audience than on stage."

The lanky, bespectacled performer broke into television in the 1960s, using the title the Amazing Kreskin. Deeply influenced by Dunninger—he even adopted the elder performer's habit of doodling on a note pad while receiving psychic impressions—Kreskin also made good use of an effect patterned after that of another stage psychic, Franz J. Polgar.

The Hungarian-born Polgar, though nev-

At a Las Vegas casino, a relieved Kreskin plucks his paycheck from its hiding place in the seat lining of a car. The mentalist had promised to surrender the fee if psychic impulses failed to guide him to the check.

er as well known as Dunninger or Kreskin, had a dramatic flair that rivaled both. A consummate muscle reader, the short, gray-haired magician undertook in 1950 to locate a small silver money clip hidden on one of the 102 floors of the Empire State Building. Linked to a volunteer guide by a mere handkerchief, Polgar found the clip within a safe in the skyscraper's basement.

Later, he developed the effect that would fire the imagination of Kreskin. Before each performance, a committee would hide Polgar's paycheck somewhere in the theater, obliging the mentalist to find it psychically or forfeit his fee. Over the years, this test pressed Polgar to the very limits of his ability. Once, he discovered the check sealed inside a tennis ball. On another occasion, a Texas police chief slipped the rolled-up check into the barrel of his revolver.

In Kreskin's hands, the paycheck routine became the stuff of national drama. A fixture on television talk shows and later the star of his own program, the blindfolded Kreskin would take one end of a handkerchief held by a volunteer and frantically hunt through studio audiences in search of his check, darting to and fro until—usually just before a commercial break—he would fall upon the

Franz J. Polgar contemplates the Empire State Building as he prepares to find a money clip hidden inside. The Hungarian mentalist found the clip in a locksmith's subbasement office.

Israeli performer Uri Geller (left), shown at the 1977 Congress for Parapsychology in Genoa, Italy, has won the admiration of audiences and the ire of most scientists with his affirmations of mystic powers.

concealed check with a triumphant cry. The effect never failed to win applause and yield future bookings.

A friendly, engaging performer, Kreskin deftly sidestepped a large part of the controversy that had surrounded Dunninger by remaining vague about the source of his ability. Asked how he accomplished an especially dazzling mind-reading effect, Kreskin told an interviewer, "I would love to tell you how I do it, but I honestly don't know."

On another occasion, when he was asked whether he could lift a heavy object with the force of his brain waves, Kreskin was even more blunt: "No," he answered, "that would be magic."

A Simple Twist of Plate

Even as Kreskin chatted amiably on America's television screens, a young Israeli was preparing to take the scientific world by storm. In a few short years, Uri Geller, known as the psychic boy wonder, would skyrocket to global renown, leaving a trail of broken spoons, twisted keys, and quarreling scientists in his wake.

Born to a Hungarian family in 1946, Geller often claims that his psychic powers first manifested themselves after he received a severe electrical shock when he was five years old. By 1969, Geller began to exhibit feats of telepathy and psychokinesis in Israeli night clubs and on kibbutzim. Finding his talents underappreciated in his own country, where some critics accused him of fraud, Geller tried his luck in the United States.

Geller succeeded when the prestigious Stanford Research Institute, a scientific think tank in Menlo Park, California, included him in its ongoing psychic investigations. Although the results were sketchy and inconclusive, Geller's apparent abilities excited the investigators and conferred a legitimacy on the performer that made his name a household word.

The bulk of his fame came to rest on the so-called Geller Effect—a display of psychokinetic strength in which the young Israeli appeared to break spoons in half, bend house keys, even halt cable cars in midair. But the entertainer also proved adept at displays of mind reading and thought projection. For one researcher, Geller duplicated a pencil sketch of a sailboat despite the artist's attempt to shield it from him. For another, he

Geller's nemesis, magician James Randi, has taken on Houdini's task of debunking psychic claims. He says most, if not all, psychics are only conjurers.

projected his own image onto photographic film seemingly by pressing his forehead against the capped lens of a camera.

In the early 1970s, it appeared that Geller had found the acceptance and respectability that had eluded his predecessors. However, he was not long on this pedestal. Like Bishop, the Zancigs, and Lady Wonder, Geller was to face his harshest criticism at the hands of a professional magician.

In 1973, Geller agreed to display his talents at the editorial offices of *Time*. Posing as a reporter, magician James Randi, a well-respected escape artist, observed Geller's effects at close quarters.

An accomplished mentalist in his own right, Randi took issue with Geller's claims. The endorsements that Geller had won from scientists meant nothing to the magician, who felt that scholars, believing themselves too smart to be fooled, were easily swayed by tricksters. When Geller completed his demonstration for the magazine's editors and left their offices, Randi promptly repeated every one of the young performer's effects.

To duplicate simple pencil sketches, Randi explained, Geller could have used a technique called pencil reading. Even if the person making the sketch held the pad out of sight, Geller would be able to recreate it by carefully tracking and then duplicating the movements of the artist's hand and pencil.

Similarly, Geller's celebrated key-warping feats were readily explained. Geller, said Randi, merely buckled the key against a tabletop.

Owing to Randi's influence, the magazine article that was subsequently published about Geller was considerably less flattering than it might otherwise have been. From that point forward, wherever Uri Geller went, James Randi seemed to follow close behind. When Geller appeared on one television show, Randi was there to supervise the conditions to preclude fraud. When Geller did mind-reading stunts, Randi improved on them. Although Geller's reputation in the United States has faded as a result, the Israeli mentalist maintains that Randi is merely a clever magician who has mimicked his results but not his methods. The effects are no less genuine, Geller says, for having been copied by trickery.

The two men seem likely to remain at odds for some time, the latest combatants in the struggle launched by Washington Irving Bishop a century ago. Perhaps the sagest words on the subject are those of Sydney and Lesley Piddington, an Australian thought-transference team popular in the 1950s. They ended their performances with a simple maxim: "Judge for yourselves."

PICTURE CREDITS

The sources for the pictures in this booklet are listed below. Credits from left to right are separated by semicolons; credits from top to bottom are separated by dashes.

Cover: Art by Lloyd K. Townsend—from *Description de l'Egypte*, Commision des Sciences et Arts, Imprimerie Impériale, 1809-1828, Paris, courtesy Bibliothèque Nationale, Paris. 3: Art by Stephen R. Wagner. 5: Art by Rebecca Butcher. 6: Scala, Florence, courtesy Museo Civico, Piacenza. 7: © Eric Valli. 8: From *Fire and Ice: A History of Comets in Art*, by Roberta M. Olson, Walker & Company, New York. 10,11: Harald Sund © 1979 Time-Life Books B.V., from *The Great Cities: Mexico City*. 12: Roger Viollet, Paris. 14,15: Tom Tracy, courtesy U.S. Geological Survey, © 1982 Time-Life Books Inc., from *Planet Earth: Earthquakes*. 16: Stone Routes, London. 17: AP/Wide World Photos. 19: Ann Ronan Picture Library, Taunton, Somerset. 20: Werner Forman Archive/British Museum, London. 21: Ashmolean Museum, Oxford. 23: Larry Sherer, courtesy Olde Towne Gemstones. 25: Art by Kathleen Bober, detail from page 29. 26-31: Art by Kathleen Bober. 32-34: Courtesy Nathaniel Altman. 35: Ceil O'Neil, detail from page 36—alphabet provided by Macmillan Publishing Company/Palmer Method Handwriting. 36,37: Ceil O'Neil—alphabet provided by Macmillan Publishing Company/Palmer Method Handwriting. 38,39: Alphabet provided by Macmillan Publishing Company/Palmer Method Handwriting. 41-45: Art by Kimmerle Milnazik. 46,47: Dice by John F. Schmidt, ovals by John Drummond. 48,49: Art by John F. Schmidt. 51: Art by Jack Pardue. 52-57: Art by Wendy Popp. 58,59: Art by Jeffrey Adams. 61: Art by Alfred T. Kamajian. 63: Henry Groskinsky. 64: Courtesy Inigo Swann. 66,67: Mary Evans Picture Library, London/Society for Psychical Research. 68,69: Edgar Cayce Foundation. 70-79: Kay Ritchie, London. 81: Theater Arts Library, Harry Ransom Humanities Research Center, University of Texas at Austin. 82: From *Confidences d'un Prestidiqitateur* by Jean Eugene Robert-Houdin, Lecesne, 1858, Blois, courtesy Bibliothèque Nationale, Paris. 83: Courtesy New York Public Library. 84: Dick Stevens, courtesy Robert Lund, American Museum of Magic; courtesy C. McCord Purdy. 85,86: Dick Stevens, courtesy Robert Lund, American Museum of Magic. 87: Mary Evans Picture Library, London/Harry Price Collection, University of London. 88: UPI/Bettmann; Milbourne Christopher Collection—Harry Price Collection, University of London. 89: Harry Price Collection, University of London. 90: Courtesy Henry Gris. 92: Dick Stevens, courtesy Robert Lund, American Museum of Magic. 93: John Vachon; courtesy Kreskin. 94: Dufoto, Rome. 95: Courtesy James Randi. Back cover: Duane Michals.